THE LIGHTER SIDE OF LIFE

THE LIGHTER SIDE OF LIFE

Humorous anecdotes and stories from an uncommon-sense perspective

Toileture™ Series — Book one

J. Christopher Eigel

Liberty Hill Press

Liberty Hill Press
2301 Lucien Way #415
Maitland, FL 32751
407.339.4217
www.libertyhillpublishing.com

Toileture™
[toi-lit-CHər] noun
Literature in short form that can read during one sitting.

Printed in the United States of America.

ISBN-13: 978-1-54566-714-9

This book is dedicated to:

My lifelong muse and mate, sounding board and editor—my acquiescing, but loving wife, Maureen.

Also, to my children, Jack and Maddie, who are throughout these stories, with whom so much humor would never have ensued, and who take it all in stride.

Table of Contents

Introduction

Congratulations and thank you for purchasing this book. It is a conglomeration of anecdotes throughout my life that struck me as either too humorous not to share or just good stories that, I hope, many folks can relate to. I have many more where these came from, so look for Book Two in the Toileture™ Series around the bend. *Toileture* is a term I have coined for this series of books and others defined as: Literature in short form that can be read during one sitting.

Many of these stories stemmed from snippets in an unusual Christmas letter I have put out to family and friends over the last two decades. Be on the lookout for *The Eigel Christmas Epistles— The Rest...of the story.*

While some might say I embellish a bit, all of the basis for the tales in this book are true—most are told with a bent towards sarcasm and should be read as such. If there was a sarcasm font available, it would be replete throughout.

I do not, nor will I, temper my stories with political correctness. So, enjoy and take no offense, for certainly none is intended. If we cannot laugh without being so easily offended, then do we really laugh at all? I end every anecdote, story, and observation with a quote from someone far more famous than me. Here are a few that I hope will help the reader understand the tone:

"Life is short, break the rules. Forgive quickly, kiss slowly. Love truly. Laugh uncontrollably. And never regret anything that makes you smile."
[Mark Twain ~ 1835–1910 ~ American Author]

"There is a thin line that separates laughter and pain, comedy and tragedy, humor and hurt."
[Erma Bombeck ~ 1927–1996 ~ American Journalist]

"If you find it hard to laugh at yourself, I would be happy to do it for you."
[Groucho Marx ~ 1895–1977 ~ American Comedian]

"Everything is funny, as long as it's happening to someone else."
[Will Rogers ~ 1879–1935 ~ American Actor]

"A day without laughter is a day wasted."
[Charlie Chaplin ~ 1888–1977 ~ English Actor]

—Chapter One—

The Honeymoon—1988

Maureen & Chris on "Tour" ~ March, 1988

I t was thirty years ago, as of March 19, 2018, when I married my wife, Maureen, and we went on our honeymoon. Spring of 1988; it was a simpler time. We were young and in love, flowers were fully in bloom in Georgia and bliss was in the air. Our whole lives were ahead of us. After all the planning and coordinating for our wedding and 400+ guests, we were ready to take a week—just the two of us. And it was going to be ***perfect***.

Well, perfect on the somewhat frugal side. My Dad was a master negotiator and consummate deal maker. There was nothing off-limits to getting a deal, in his world. I once watched him try to negotiate the price of a Burger King Whopper to match a McDonald's Big Mac. That fourteen-year-old cashier never recovered.

So, Dad got us a deal on our stay in Acapulco, Mexico. Someone at the office had a timeshare condo swap-out that he traded a week's vacation for, at a discount of course, and threw in some travel voucher coupons for free nuts and a reduced-alcohol content drink at the airport bar (buy-one get-one). Maureen was leery of any deal through my Dad, we'd dated four and a half years, so she knew his proclivities, but everything looked nice in the brochure and having made it through the large wedding, we were looking forward to just chilling.

As you fly in and out of Acapulco, Mexico… it's very brown. There is one spot of green you can see as you descend from cruising altitude, and that belongs to one exclusive resort—the Acapulco Princess Mundo Imperial. The resort's centerpiece is a magnificent, fifteen-story Aztec-style pyramid framed by the modern Princess and Pearl Towers and is surrounded by 480 hectares of lush gardens and swaying palm trees. Incredible. Other than that, the country looks pretty much like desert.

We arrived in our new honeymoon clothes, Maureen was beautiful in a white lace Mexican sundress. I was sporting white cotton pants and a Tommy Bahama shirt, topped by a straw, wide-brimmed Panama Jack style hat that said "Acapulco," on the band above the brim. Very suave. We took a discount passenger van to the condo, that had a few stops, of which ours was the last one, but it was a great deal. We looked lovingly in each other's eyes as the other passengers were dropped at their destinations. The first stop was the Princess, and wow, was it majestic. Waterfalls cascading through the lobby, flamingos ambling about, vivid flowers, and lush grass. Beautiful.

Then each drop-off after that was, less and less spectacular. We wound down through the streets approaching Acapulco Bay, which, from a distance, was picturesque. But as we drove by the local beach, where we hoped to saunter arm in arm on a romantic walk, it was pretty destitute. Dirty children were begging beachgoers for coins. Most folk were dressed in well-worn frocks from the 70s. Yeah...I'd classify it as extremely poor and it looked a little unsafe. We kept on our positive smiles, even as the conversation all but stopped, and that loving sparkle started waning from Maureen's eyes. We turned away from the beach and wound up the side of a mountain to arrive at the condo.

It wasn't dirty. It wasn't the Acapulco Princess, but it looked okay and it was our honeymoon—we were together, that's what mattered. It could still be mostly perfect. We checked in and got the key to the condo. As the elevator came to our floor, it didn't quite line up. We sort of had to step up out of the elevator five or six inches onto the landing. Okay, this could happen anywhere. I didn't dare look into Maureen's eyes, because I knew the sparkle was lost in welling tears. We got to the room, how bad could this be?

It turns out we didn't really need the key, the door was slightly ajar. Good thing I peeked in first, because as I turned on the lights, a small rodent scurried out of sight. I think it was a Mexican mouse, but no cute yellow sombrero and no "Ándele, arriba!" Definitely not Speedy Gonzales. Just a bad omen.

3

No one had put out fresh flowers, which would have helped stifle the fetor from the refrigerator with its door cracked open and reeking of something rotting or curdled, or both. Now came the tears. I turned to Maureen, who had backed up several steps, was clutching her bag tight against her chest and shaking her head from side to side—before I could even quip to lighten the mood, she implored shakily, "I can't stay here. I want to stay at the Princess." *Perfect.*

So, we went back to the lushest resort in all of Mexico and had the honeymoon we'd always dreamed of and couldn't afford. It was all-inclusive, five swimming pools with swim-up bars, lobster and steak dinners, a protected beachfront, guarded against local riff-raff; absolutely incredible. And with no flights available to shorten the stay and avoid cleaning out my savings, we spent a week in paradise. And it was paradise. We settled easily into the lap of luxury, took a couple of cool Jeep tours and ended up having a fantastic time.

In hindsight, I wouldn't have traded it for the world. But I would have taken a discount.

"Life is short, break the rules. Forgive quickly, kiss slowly. Love truly. Laugh uncontrollably. And never regret anything that makes you smile."
[Mark Twain ~ 1835–1910 ~ American Author]

Chapter Two

Valentine's Day—1989

At our first house in Tucker, GA ~ circa 1989

A nniversaries are a bit of an enigma for me. I think about them
often as they approach, and then seem to, without fail, forget
them the actual day they arrive. Not sure exactly why that is, but
nonetheless, it is. To illustrate the point, and not something I am
particularly proud of, but on our first Valentine's Day as a married
couple, failure was inevitable.

Setting the scene: going back to 1989, when the first of many anniversary tests was approaching, it was an omen of things to come. It was not a wedding anniversary or birthday, although, sadly those eventually would fall into this ignoble pattern, but Valentine's Day; the one day to express your undying love—and the first one to be shared with my new wife, Maureen. We were living in a small town north of Atlanta, and it was a Tuesday.

I was young (some would interject "and stupid" here), working hard, long hours and we had dated for almost five years before we married. The trifecta for not realizing the significance of specific calendar related dates. Young = oblivious, hardworking = focus on the big picture (meaning life, not Hallmark holidays), and almost five years of dating = comfort in our relationship—never mind it was our first married Valentine's Day. Not sure how *that's* important.

I remember it like it was yesterday. I was running late to a dinner at Maureen's parents' house. She had called to suggest we meet over at her parents for dinner at 7 p.m.—which sounded great, since her Mother was an excellent cook. But, as usual, I was running late and hustling towards her folk's house so I wouldn't be late-as-usual. Gary McKee, a local DJ on 94Q, a popular music station back in the day, was going on about something or other when I heard the words "...and I hope you haven't forgotten today is Valentine's Day!" I am not the swiftest study in the world, but even I could put two and two together. A hastily-arranged dinner with her folks on a Tuesday and it was the 14th of February. That spelled out, in little pink sugar hearts, t-r-o-u-b-l-e.

So, not to be totally empty-handed, even though I was almost to their house and already a few minutes late, I whipped into the local Kroger, where Valentine's cards should be in abundance. I did not consider chocolates or flowers, even though this was our first such day in our married lives, because I had already established in our five years of courtship that such foresight should not be expected and certainly not in a last-minute dinner invite. So, I ran to the card section where there were—all of two cards left. Total. And both were "To My Husband."

I am sure anyone seeing me run in, peruse the selection and then witness what must have been a look of total dejection, would have both known instantly my predicament and been amused and saddened at the same time. Alas.

I had no choice. I took the more sincere of the two and went to the checkout line. The woman there glanced at the card in mild disgust... mixed with a curious eyebrow raised. I explained, "I'm not gay (not that there's anything wrong with that!), I'm just running late to my In-Laws' for dinner with my wife for Valentine's Day and I have a plan!"

"Umm-hmm. Bless your heart."

"Bless your heart" is a phrase that is common in the Southern United States. The phrase has multiple meanings. It can be used as a sincere expression of sympathy or genuine concern. It can be used as a precursor to an insult to soften the blow. It is also sometimes used to mean "you are dumb or otherwise impaired, but you can't help it" by individuals who wish to "be sweet" and do not wish to "act ugly". The latter meaning applied in this case.

As I walked into the house some twenty minutes late, Maureen, her Mom and Dad happened to be standing in the kitchen and were looking expectantly in my direction. Even though we were recently married, we had been dating long enough for me to know that these types of dates held a certain level of meaning and expectation and should not be forgotten. All this introspection was not lost on me at my young age.

I pulled the card from behind my back and proclaimed somewhat sheepishly I had not forgotten Valentine's Day, as I handed it to her. Her folks looked relieved that they would not be witness to another disappointment caused by me, for their only daughter. While I think they were somewhat surprised that I actually had anything, they were hesitant to heap any praise on me just yet. She opened the card. Everywhere it had said "husband" I crossed out and wrote in "wife" making it the *perfect* Valentine's card.

Crisis ~~averted~~ *delayed*.

It went something like this:

> To my loving ~~Husband~~, *Wife*
> *you are the beginning and the end.*
> As your ~~Wife~~, *Husband* I will love and cherish
> you as a ~~Husband~~ *Wife* should be cherished,
> *for all the days of our lives.*
>
> *Love now and forever,*
> *Your* ~~Wife~~ *Husband*
>
> ## Chris

Maureen threw back her 80s hair as she laughed a good laugh and then shook her head knowingly and sighed. She is, categorically, the best of spouses and, while I know to this day she still pines for a more romantic mate, she knew what she was getting. She sacrificed and married me anyway—and has made her peace with it, I'm pretty sure...after all we've had an incredible thirty plus years. Which means I've done something right, right? And which also means there's something I should probably go ahead and get on the calendar for next year?

"Love the man who promises the least; he'll be the least disappointing."
[Bernard Baruch ~ 1870–1965 ~ American businessman]

—Chapter Three—

Grandpa and Baseball—1991

Knucksie doing the Tomahawk Chop...Jim rocking a mullet...Brave's at attention...Maureen & Me in a rally cap with Ernest L Martin ~ from the 1991 family photo album

Last century, back in the 1980s and early 90s, before the corruption of sports by leftist agendas and millionaire athletes who would strike for more millions, I had a purest love for professional baseball and was a huge fan. If you lived in the southeast from 1991 through 2005, the Brave's fan base was legion and as devoted as any during Atlanta's unprecedented run of fourteen consecutive Division Championships.

My Grandfather was eighty-six years old in 1991. Born in 1905, he was one of seven children, who grew up on a farm in rural Illinois just outside of Danville and finished high school in a graduating class of nine. Instead of accepting a horse and buggy for graduation, he asked his father for money to offset a loan to pay for college and worked for four years before enrolling at Mt. Morris in 1927.

He walked onto the football team there, having to watch others put their equipment on to learn how to don the uniform, but quickly became a first-string tackle. He lettered in football, baseball, basketball, and track, and then was recruited to play starting tackle for the University of Illinois where he graduated with a degree in Mechanical Engineering.

He was married in 1932, faithfully for sixty-five years, until my grandmother died at eighty-seven in 1997. He'd seen the advent of broadcast radio, motion pictures, even zippers. Lived through two World Wars, the Great Depression, saw mankind make it to the moon and return safely…the list goes on and on. They moved to Hoopeston, Illinois in the 30s and had two daughters: my Aunt Karen and four years later, my Mom.

Karen would be on the first-ever cheerleading squad at the University of Illinois, and my Mom was a cheerleader in high school for the Hoopeston Corn Jerkers. Not even kidding here. Back in the day, you shucked, or jerked, the husk off ears of corn from the plentiful cornfields of rural Illinois, so that was what their team name was. One of the defensive cheers went "Jerk 'em back, jerk 'em back, waaaaaay back!"

The PC police might squash that kind of verbiage this day and age, but back then it was just cheering. Grandpa walked to work every day, weather permitting, and provided for his family. He was a moral man from a different era—what a great time to be alive.

In the late 1980s, I followed, not only major league baseball, but minor league teams too, scouted players for my own edification, was in a rotisserie baseball league—*not* to be confused with fantasy baseball, either! In fantasy baseball, you simply draft the best players in a couple of hours and build your team based solely on talent, no worry about salaries or player value or strategy in how to fill out positions on your team.

In rotisserie baseball, it's like you're managing an actual team; each owner has a salary cap to stay within, trade value, starting and backup positions to fill. All this was done at a grueling day-long draft with the eleven other owners, bidding against each other for players based on their real stats from the 162-game season. It was total dork-ness, but it was awesome!

I had been following the Braves for years, and practically worshiped the old legends: Bob Horner, Phil Niekro, Glen Hubbard, and Dale Murphy. Murph was pulling down about $2 million, which was out of this world in 1987, and these nobody pitchers named Glavine and Smoltz were making about $65,000 each. In 1990, I knew something special was about to be unleashed.

My Dad and I were in business together at the time, and in 1990, the Braves were in dead-last place. But I saw this incredible talent coming up—Steve Avery, Ron Gant, Tommy Glavine, David Justice, Greg Olson, Alejandro Pena, John Smoltz, Mark Wohlers and this young buck named Chipper Jones. Bobby Cox was at the helm, and I knew they were on the cusp.

13

I talked my Dad into buying season tickets, even though they were in last place. We got a great deal, eleven rows behind the Braves' dugout and watched them go from worst to first and start that historical run of fourteen consecutive Division Championships and four World Series appearances, finally wining in 1995.

That year, when they went from worst to first, and to the World Series for the first time since 1958, we watched every pitch, screamed and danced when they won the playoffs in dramatic fashion, and we had first shot at season ticket seats for the World Series...which of course, we took! We were very popular with clients and friends that year.

I took for granted the ability to go to Major League ballgames. Years earlier, I would occasionally buy two-dollar outfield tickets when the Braves were awful, and along with the other 2,200 patrons, would just move behind home plate and watch the games from there. But with season tickets in-hand, I had been to many of the home games during the '91 season.

And here, my eighty-six-year-old Grandfather had never been to any professional baseball game. Spending hard earned money for something as gratuitous as a baseball game? It was not a priority. But he had watched baseball religiously on TV and was an avid Braves fan. When I found out he'd never been to a major league game, Maureen, my brother Jim, and I decided, not only was he going to sit in awesome seats in a major league stadium, but he was going to sit in those seats for game five of the 1991 World Series.

I wanted him to see it all. We got to Atlanta Fulton County Stadium, walked through the Braves Hall of Fame, ordered popcorn and hotdogs, and he got the whole experience along with 52,000 other fans. Hall of Famer, Phil "Knucksie" Niekro threw out the first pitch—a knuckle ball, of course. The National Anthem was sung proudly, and *all* the players stopped what they were doing, put their hands over their hearts and faced the flag. Fireworks went off at "the bombs bursting in air," and a flyover by the Blue Angels was spectacular. He was amazed to see this all live and in person. To be an eighty-six-year-old at his *first* baseball game, which was also game five of the World Series... how incredibly cool was that? I still get a catch in my throat thinking about it.

The Brave's won the game, fourteen to five, and Grandpa had to be in seventh heaven! I'm not sure I'll ever know how much he really enjoyed that day, because he was a quiet man who spoke little. He was John Wayne, without the flash, ramrod straight posture, and bigger than life. As one of my favorite country singers, Randy Travis, lyric opines, *He wore starched white shirts, buttoned at the neck. And I thought he walked on water.* He was a loyal husband, a great dad, and the grandfather you couldn't help but respect. I don't believe he ever made it to another game; he died in 2000, at ninety-five years old. But I'll never forget October 24, 1991, when my Grandfather saw his first major league baseball game, in person at the ballpark.

The picture of him below was maybe the first selfie ever taken, albeit in a mirror. He took this with his new Zeiss Ikoflex 75mm Tessler in 1940-something and developed it in his own darkroom down in his basement. Love this old pic and kept his old camera he took it with—which probably still works, if you could buy film for it.

Ernest L Martin and his Zeiss Ikoflex ~ circa 1940-something

"Love is the most important thing in the world, but baseball is pretty good, too."
[Yogi Berra ~ 1925–2015 ~ American Athlete]

—Chapter Four—

The Slug-bug Massacre; October 13—1991

Slug-bug blue pickup! Slug-bug Batmobile! Slug-bug Convertible! Slug-bug Rolls Royce!

I grew up with three brothers; one older and two younger. There are many stories of fist-to-cuffs and typical picking at each other as brothers are prone to do. Nothing too serious beyond broken light bulbs over heads, fat lips, bruised ribs, broken doors, holes in sheetrock walls and shattered windows... normal stuff. See, back

17

in the day we didn't have mindless video games to teach us violence; we had to learn it firsthand...

We played outside after school and during the summers and had to be home when the sun went down—to an unlocked house. We either ran where we needed to go, or when older, rode a bike or skateboard and without helmets because I don't even think they were invented yet, unless you rode a motorcycle. If they were, we didn't own any.

Of course, my brother Tim ended up in a semi-coma for two days and blew out an eardrum leaving him mostly deaf in one ear when he slammed into a tree, biking through a wet lawn when he was ten... so maybe helmets for kids were a good invention? We were pretty rough and tumble and decent fighters; if you picked on one of us, you got all of us.

But we weren't allowed to fight in the car. Mostly because my Dad reaching back from over the front seat to try and grab one of us, while keeping one hand on the wheel was just too unsafe. That wasn't the only thing unsafe, seat-belt laws weren't mandated until 1988 in Georgia and growing up in the late 70's, we never wore seat belts in the back seat —I'm not even sure the car had them... Turning around to smack one of us while driving occasionally caused the car to swerve and one of us would slam into the door to the great amusement of the others.

On any kind of a curve in the road, we would put our feet against the door and push as hard as we could in an attempt to squish the other two or three brothers against the far door. Based on which way the curve went, with nine years between us, there was a distinct weight advantage, especially if centrifugal force was on your side. That inevitably led to lines being "drawn" on the seat, which we couldn't cross without serious repercussions from our parents, so we had to resort to nonphysical games. But games like the alphabet game and I-Spy weren't too stimulating to four boys and grew irksome fast (especially for my brothers, because I always won).

One of the "games" we used to play that combined the optical sense, conversing with each other and the all-important punching, was called Slug-bug. Slug-bug was a game born of desperation to be both vigilant and engaged with your surroundings and still encompass an acceptable level of physical exertion. A "Bug" was actually a classic Volkswagen Beetle, which affectionately attained its name from the 1968 Disney movie; *Herbie the Love Bug*.

© 1968 Herbie the Love Bug ~ Walt Disney Motion Pictures

Here's how it worked: If you were the first one to spot a VW Beetle or "Bug", you got to slug one of your brothers —usually in the upper arm, but occasionally a thigh shot would do when the arm was bruised. When you spotted it, you called Slug-bug and the color; "Slug-bug red!" and earned your right to pop the kid next to

19

you. Others have called this punch buggy, but in the spirit of Disney and Herbie, we went with Slug-bug...

As we got older and could really hurt each other, we pretty quickly grew out of the physical aspect Slug-bug and modified it to a points system. This was still engaging and refreshingly non-bruising. And punching someone several years younger only landed you in trouble anyway.

The South was replete with VW Beetles in the 1970's and 80's, so it was a pretty active game wherever we went. The family also took a couple of trips each year to Panama City Beach (affection-ally referred to as the Redneck Riviera) and there was a plethora of Bugs in the Panhandle of Florida!

There were all kinds of Bugs, some in abundance and some pretty scarce. You had standard hardtop Bugs and convertible Bugs of course, but then people got a little crazy and put Rolls Royce hoods on the fronts. Some converted the backs to pick-up beds. There were even novelty bugs like the Batmobile-bug and the extremely rare Rolls Royce pickup-bug. So, we devised a points system, and played for score.

1pt – Slug-bug [color]
2pts – Slug-bug [color] Convertible
3pts – Slug-bug Dune-bug (Panama City Beach localized —mostly)
5pts – Slug-bug Pick-up
7pts – Slug-bug Rolls-Royce
15pts – Slug-bug Rolls-Royce pickup truck
(we only saw one of these in all the years we played, establishing the point value on the fly)

By the time my youngest brother Jim was driving (legally) in 1987, we had pretty much outgrown the game and would only play it if we were all together on the way to a golf outing while down in the Redneck Riviera or something... Plus, the Beetle, with its rear-mounted, air-cooled-engine, was banned in America for failing to meet safety and emission standards in 1977. Worldwide sales of the car shrank by the late 1970s and by 1988, the classic Beetle was sold only in Mexico. So, we didn't see as many of them around anymore.

But we'd still play on occasion, and this was a topic of discussion in late 1991 when my Aunt Bonnie, Uncle Jay and two cousins stayed with my wife and me for a big Eigel wedding. At the time, we lived in a little area in the far northern burbs of Atlanta called Hickory Flat. They had adopted the same point system and we had played Slug-bug intra-family when we saw each other over the years.

Whenever they came south from Chicago, there were more Bugs to be spotted around Atlanta and it gave the families a fun game to play. Over the years, this grew to a friendly rivalry between the northern Eigels and the southern contingent, each claiming dominance and superior skills. Of course, we stayed a little sharper with the Florida connection, but even comments such as those were mock points of contention.

Uncle Jay and Aunt Bonnie were (and are) great to have as guests; Jay would bring his guitar–the family is musically talented, and Bonnie was always laughing her infectious laugh, and their two kids, Matt (fifteen) and Emily (twelve) clearly looked up to me as the older and wiser cousin back in 1991. Ahem.

On the way down to a get-together with the rest of the extended family, we decided to play the Slug-bug game. They had a

21

[Northern] rule where you had to give ten seconds notice when starting the game so everyone was prepared and couldn't be blind-sided by having the game start with cheap points scored.

As we started the game, the Northern Eigel's suspicions were heightened that there was something afoot, since I was driving. But a Slug-bug or two were spotted and Jay may have even been up a point or two. Their guard was down when I took a winding road, cornering between two buildings to a stop sign, where across the street sat a Slug-bug graveyard.

They never saw it coming. There were Slug-bugs galore! On blocks. On flatbeds. Long grass growing up around several. Rusted. New. Old. Every color of the rainbow. I launched into the game like a Gatling gun in a knife fight. Slug-bug red! Slug-bug green! Slug-bug blue convertible! Slug-bug gold! Slug-bug white! Slug-bug red convertible! —you get the idea... and the dreaded Slug-bug pick-up truck was sitting there as a bonus, driving the final nail in the Slug-bug coffin.

They didn't even score a point. Jay tried feebly but he was tracking a few seconds behind and then went into a sort of catatonic shock. Matt was screaming about rules infractions and the brutality in a friendly game, while Emily started to cry and ask how I could do this to *family* and Bonnie roared with laughter. It was a mas-sacre. They were an unsuspecting and trusting lot —surely no rel-ative would take them down in such an underhanded and fiendish fashion. I thought it was all in great jest, but it was kind of an uncomfortable ride the rest of the way...

They never stayed with us in Hickory Flat again. We talked about it in hushed tones only recently, some two and a half decades later. It's still a little soon.

To this day, you can't really bring it up with Uncle Jay – he becomes very sullen; he can't even say "bug" anymore (he uses "insect"). And he lobbied against the VW manufacture of the new Beetle in 1998 siting PTSBD [*Post Traumatic Slug-bug Disorder*]...

Matt has a *twitch* that resurfaces when he sees a Slug-bug of any color; we've found it best not to call that twitch a "tick" —too close to "bug". He's attended years of anger management therapy at no small expense...

Emily had blocked all memory of the "incident" completely (she was young when the atrocity occurred), until we relived it recently at a family reunion, which enlightened her as to why she always tears-up when she sees actual slugs... She commented recently; "How could you? You were older, and wiser"...

Aunt Bonnie; she still laughs (maybe a little to hysterically) the same as she did the day of the massacre every time she sees a classic VW Beetle –especially a convertible...

As for me, I smile ruefully whenever I see one of the Love Bug movies in the cable TV guide, or chuckle lightly when I actually see one in person. In his refusal to endorse this book, Uncle Jay sighted this chapter, stating, "I am still not able to talk about in any serious way. The pain is still too much. The hardest thing to deal with is the gleeful, underhanded way you set it up. Another problem that you noted is that our children took years to "get right". Is there a statute of limitations on assault with a slug-bug? Reopening the wound this summer, and then here in front of God and everybody, is so surprising and hurtful in so many ways. Blood thicker than water? ...yeah right!"

In theory there is no difference between theory and practice.
In practice there is.
[Yogi Berra ~ 1925–2015 ~ American Athlete]

—Chapter Five—

I Should Have Yelled Two!—1993

© 1980 Caddyshack

G olf is a funny sport. Not funny in the humorous way—
although it certainly can be. It is a game of precision and
fractions: inches, trajectory, speed, rhythm, timing, and balance.
All these things must be in sync to strike a ball flush and send
it the desired distance, to the desired destination. Funny in a
capricious way.

A lot of you who don't golf, may wonder why us amateurs go out and do something so frustrating and that we so obviously will never master. Part of it is the challenge, part of it is we hit the exact same shots you see the Pros hit on TV—we just don't hit them consecutively or with any consistency, but we do hit them. I've dropped in Eagles from 150 yds and sunk sixty-five-foot snaking putts, I've hit miracle chips into the hole from a greenside bunker, and driven the ball over 300 yards many times, and not downhill off the cart-path either. That's what keeps us amateurs coming back.

My father, older brother Keith, and I used to sneak nine holes in every Tuesday before work at a local course in Atlanta: Chastain Golf Course. They called it their Early Bird Special and we would get the first tee time so we could scoot around in about an hour and a half. We weren't great golfers back then, nor are we now. But we thought we could be, and hope is all there is when you're a hacker. I think I was about a fifteen index in those years—shooting in the mid-nineties.

On this particular day, a buddy of ours, Will Starnes, and I shared a cart; we usually put my dad in the other cart because he was a ball hunter. This enabled him to drive precariously close to water hazards where he would trundle along scouting for other's golf balls—long lost and forgotten. The official limit of clubs in the bag is fourteen, but we always allowed the ball retriever as an extra club, and my Dad had one of those fifteen-foot extension babies that he worked as deftly as a master swordsman—occasionally not even exiting the cart while retrieving a submerged ball. I think he used it enough to have it re-gripped.

On this particular day, I don't recall whether I was hitting the ball great or poorly, but we were moving around the course in good fashion. We found ourselves on the number eight tee box, it's now the seventeenth hole: a 491-yard par five. The tee is dramatically elevated, the fairway narrow off the box and a lay-up hole, because at the bottom is deep and fast-moving Nancy Creek, crossing the fairway, which is walled within a twenty foot deep cement canal. The creek is about 230 yds to reach and 280 to carry.

So, with the downhill, the club for me was a five-iron — a club that I could control and that if struck properly would leave me a solid three-wood, in those days it was actually wood, not metal as the clubs are today, into the green for my Eagle putt. I knew this hole like the back of my hand. Unfortunately, the hole knew me as well. Running the length of the left side of the hole is Powers Ferry Road.

The previous week I had my trusty five-iron out and put a smooth stroke on the ball. But, as can happen to the best of us, my hands lagged slightly behind the club-head as I swung through and, while I won't call it a duck hook (which is a ball so poorly struck, at about a hundred yards out it starts turning so hard that it goes as far left as it does forward), I call it a towering power-draw. It drew right off the hole and onto the road. Well, technically it never hit the road, but it would have if some MARTA bus hadn't gotten in the way. It hit the top of the bus with a clang — I'm sure it made a few mass transit commuters jump in their seats, as it ricocheted off into the land where golf balls go to die.

I thought about taking a bus-interference mulligan with no penalty, because had the bus not been there, it is likely the ball would have shot off the curb and come to rest back in play anyway. But being a steward of the sport, I could not, in good conscience, invoke that little-known local rule, and took my drop where the ball left the course. (We play our own version of stroke and distance... come on, it's penalty enough to have to add a stroke, but distance too?)

With that memory fresh in my mind, and once again my trusty five-iron in hand, I knew to let my hands lead and not repeat the humiliation suffered a mere week ago. I did take a quick peek to make sure no buses were in sight. Instead, I blocked the ball out to the right, and while I didn't hit a wicked slice (which is a ball so poorly struck, at about a hundred yards out it starts turning so hard that it goes as far right as it does forward), I call it a towering power-fade. Are you beginning to notice whenever the ball is miss-hit, I describe it as "towering?" That my friends, is compensation in the vernacular.

The shot drifted right and down the hill towards a giant oak—the trunk, a good twelve feet in diameter. As the golf cart skidded to a stop on the incline near the bottom of the hill, I clambered out and found my ball about three feet short of the base of the tree. This put the giant oak between the green and me.

My only option was to aim way left, towards that road those menacing buses drive on, and hit a looping power-fade across Nancy Creek, so I still would have a chance to reach the green in three and two-putt for par. A little knockdown eight-iron with a dash of magic is what was needed. I put a good swing on the shot and avoided the hazard and kept it inbounds in the left rough leaving about 190 yards to the pin. Frankly, it was one of my better efforts.

Back to the trusty five-iron. The only concern was one of those big, round, concrete drainage culverts about forty to fifty yards ahead; but it was a minor concern because anything except an all-out scalded blade would easily be up in the air well before the culvert, which was only about eighteen inches above the ground. It would need to be a full swing and solidly struck to carry to the green. I hit it full, but thin; a badly scalded blade. That's when time drew to a crawl, like in the Matrix movies, where time nearly stands still as you can see the bullet traveling in slow-motion.

I can still see this in my mind's-eye like it was yesterday. The bladed shot, hit really "thin" off the bottom of the face of the iron, exploded forward at well over a hundred mph, but never got more than eighteen inches off the ground. In slow motion, as my club came through, and keeping my head down like you are taught in a good swing, hips rotating through the ball, the right heel coming up as the club came up over my shoulders, which were now squared up perpendicular to the trajectory of the shot, my eyes were slowly coming up, tracking the ball. The odds of it hitting the round culvert at the perfect angle to deflect the ball directly back from whence it came had to be astronomical and I'm no physicist, but it sure looked to be traveling back faster than it left.

All this happened in a split second and as the ball hurled back in a straight line at my mid-section, as my follow-through continued, all I could do was watch. Watch it come back like a rocket right into my now perfectly squared-up hips from my model rotation towards my unprotected "boys."

Even though it was all in slow-motion, there was no time to react, no time to cover up, no time do anything except, accept impact. And impact it did. Luckily, I'm a tighty-whities golfer because boxers would have left "things" dangling in harm's way. I think I was playing Top Flight's at the time and they have little compression. Not that it mattered what brand ball it was. That ball clipped the boys at about 100 mph and there was nothing but white-hot pain, and then, nothing.

The next thing I know, I'm lying in the early morning dew-covered grass in the fetal position, hands clasping my family jewels and moaning softly. My cart partner, Will, was also lying in the grass where he fell out of the cart. Apparently when you are laughing that hard, it is very difficult to keep your balance, even if you are sitting in a golf cart. Keith and my Dad looked on in shock, before also going into hysterics.

The other unfortunate sidebar is this particular shot happened to be equal distance between the tee and green of an adjacent par three and the next tee box to a par four heading away from the hole I was laying on. The course was quite full by this time, so there were no less than twelve people watching the aftermath of what I will call the most unlikely and errant shot of my career. It was impossible for them not to look over, with Will guffawing at the top of his lungs.

Well, needless to say, I didn't play the last hole. Ice from the clubhouse was the order of the day, (a cold bag of peas would have been awesome) as Dad drove us to work. He had called ahead with the news of my calamity and when I got to my office, taped to the door was a quickly drawn sketch of a golf tee with two golf balls sitting upon it...*classic*.

This happened between the births of my two children, and a few years after the first, we struggled to conceive our second. I can never be sure if this caused the damage, but I did have a bilateral varicocele repair in early 1995 to fix the plumbing... I guess the lesson is, don't ever blade a five-iron if there's a round drainage culvert forty to fifty yards ahead...I bet Hank Haney or Harvey Penick never taught that lesson—so I've got that going for me, which is nice.

"Everything is funny, as long as it's happening to someone else."
[Will Rogers ~ 1879–1935 ~ American Actor]

—Chapter Six—

You Jack-Wagon!—1993

Young Jack ~ circa 1993

Nothing about raising children is easy. There are hundreds of little things you do, that until your children are grown and raising their own, they'll never appreciate. I know that was the case with my parents and me. But, man, do I appreciate that now. They had to know a whole lot more than they ever let on—well, at least my dad did. Not so sure my mom understands, or at least acknowledges, even today, half the things my brothers and I did. Or maybe she does and is using selective memory to remember those younger years more fondly, when we still told her how much we loved her or gave her hugs for no reason at all.

As it turns out, children see and hear everything. Even things they couldn't possibly hear or were not in their line of sight, somehow are collected in their young, impressionable minds. The seeds are planted. And sooner or later, you reap what you sow. For me, as a parent, it was too often harvested for the bad, and at the wrong time, in the wrong place, with the wrong audience. Like an elderly, tea-toting Grandmother coming out of church — or worse yet, in church!

As all these little seeds of observation get planted and begin to take hold; slowly is the character of a child shaped and molded. They will hear what you say, and maybe listen, until they reach that certain age where you can say nothing they don't already know, but they will totally watch what you do, no matter what you say. Especially when they know you don't know they're watching. And even though they won't admit it or maybe even understand when it's happening, they never stop taking it in. They're like little sponges soaking it all up and unfortunately you can't wring out the bad stuff they've absorbed.

It's like the Rodney Atkins's song, Watching You:

"I've been watching you, dad, ain't that cool?
I'm your buckaroo, I wanna be like you
And eat all my food, and grow as tall as you are
We got cowboy boots and camo pants
Yeah, we're just alike, hey, ain't we dad?
I wanna do everything you do
So I've been watching you."

Early in the spring of 1993, our son, Jack, was just shy of two. We've had great experiences, and being the first child, try to capture every moment—him learning to talk, taking his first steps. He never did crawl. He used to do that Army-drag thing on his belly, then eventually found tables and chairs to pull himself up and hang on to. Then one day he went from dragging himself around to just walking upright. If I had been thinking that first year, I would have fastened a bunch of the Swiffer wipes to him and had the floor dusted. Probably could've patented that sucker; *Swiffer Jack Jammies*.

Just like the song, he'd been watching us. I'm switching the narrative to "us" now, because in all fairness, his mother spent a lot more time with him than I did. We were both working, but in those days my hours were long, and my temper was maybe a hair thin. Almost exclusively with inanimate objects, though. A lawnmower that wouldn't start might garner a choice expletive or two. A poorly-directed hammer onto an unsuspecting thumb might force a string of colorful invectives. Or a screen door that wouldn't close properly might be thoroughly tested, repeatedly, to see if the hinges or the latch were the problem with not closing, which of course necessitated some imaginative commentary. Now, I'm fairly certain little toddler Jack was nowhere near during these events, and therefore, couldn't have any of those bad seeds being planted by me.

Jack wasn't wanting for toys to play with, but he loved an old red Radio Flyer wagon we'd acquired from somewhere along the way. He'd put his stuff in that thing and pull it around all over the place. You could see gears in his mind always turning, and, after mastering walking upright, he was really just learning how to talk in complete sentences—with context. He'd ride on the tractor with me when we cut the grass, asking about the gears and blades—we lived on about one and three-quarter acres back then, and had a lot of yard. A lot. With me working so much and wanting downtime on the weekends, I may not have cut the lawn as often as it actually needed it.

One day, little Jack was pulling that wagon through the uncut yard, and there were some pretty good clumps of grass. Let's call them *tufts*. To give you perspective, we backed up to a ninety-one-acre ranch, and the cows would always come over to our back yard, because the grass was really high and easy to cowlick. They'd just reach their huge heads over the fence and twirl that gigantic tongue around my nice, long tall grass and yank it right out. So, maybe the yard was a little out of control. Anyway, I went out to check on little Jack, and he's trying to pull that wagon through some pretty tall turf and the axels are hung up.

Then it all came full circle. That sweet little curly-headed toddler let a string of cusswords go like he was a sailor in the Navy. I can't publish them here but, let me just say, he used them perfectly in context—which by the way, was impressive. But that's not the point. I turned back towards the house and hollered to Maureen to come explain what in the world kind of language she was using around our son! Yeah, like it was her.

34

Sometimes your children teach you; even when they're not yet two. I couldn't really even punish him, because he did use them correctly. All of them. Those initial seeds maybe weren't so great, but we learned and sowed good ones too and little Jack grew up and turned out okay. Mostly. I'll bet our good parenting choice of getting him exposure observing bad parenting choices, will eventually make him a good parent. At least, that's what we tell ourselves.

"Good judgment comes from experience, and a lot of that comes from bad judgment."
[Will Rogers ~ 1879–1935 ~ American Actor]

—Chapter Seven—

The Tiny Ship was
Tossed—1996

Dad & Keith on a Tack ~ circa 1996
"Just sit right back and you'll hear a tale, a tale of a fateful trip..."

B ack in the day, before a series of hurricanes culminating
in Ivan in 2004, had wiped the sand dunes of the Florida
Panhandle away. Back when you could drive your trailered catamarans and jet skis onto the beach with impunity. Before every square

inch of beachfront was packed with bodies, the Eigel clan used to live for the trips to Panama City Beach. The whole family would head down and enjoy a week in the surf and sun. Now-a-days, the free spirit and relatively lax enforcement of "beach access laws" is of a bygone era. They're still beautiful to be sure—there's nothing in the world like the white sand and clear waters of the Panhandle, but it's just not the same.

Twenty some-odd years ago, we would drive the trailers onto the beach through a public access point, rig the boats, and roll the catamarans down on big cat-tracks, which were inflatable tires designed to roll the boats thought the sand, set sail and go. My dad was a big sailor; he got his license on Lake Superior and could rig and sail just about anything. Brothers Keith and Jim were not far behind, both still masters of the craft. We'd have great runs; if the surf or wind was up, someone would be out on a broad reach or hard tack, riding on one pontoon.

When Keith and Jim sailed, they'd sheath the dagger boards (which slid through an opening in the bottom of the hulls) and sail the boats in, right up the face of the beach doing about twenty knots on one pontoon, bring them into the wind and set them down in the sand. As the beaches got more crowded, this became tougher to navigate without scaring the living bejesus out of innocent folk strolling down the beach looking for seashells. My brother Tim and I were usually along for the ride as either ballast or to work the jib (smaller forward) sail. We were also excellent beer drinkers, ready to toast the captain after a proper sail and landing.

When the wind would get up, or a storm was rolling in—that was the best sailing. We would jump those boats off the crests in five and six-foot swells and cut through the ocean. Many times, dolphins would race alongside or porpoise between the pontoons. One day in late October, a storm was rolling in and being mid-afternoon, we knew there wouldn't be too many runs left, so my dad and I decided to go for a fast run.

"The mate was a mighty sailing man, the Skipper brave and sure..."

It was fast. We were flying from crest to crest—the swells not too deep, which can make it a little hairy. We had great wind and were on a long tack heading towards the bigger swells in the shipping channel about a mile away, between the point of the beach and Shell Island, which bracketed the channel. Brother Jim was running chaser on a jet-ski, and we were having a great time. Until we weren't.

We had run about a mile-and-a half to two miles away from shore and were getting ready to come about. For the non-sailors: on a tight tack you sail about forty-five degrees off the direction of the wind, "coming about" is when you bring the boat dead into the wind to turn and run the other direction at the opposite ninety-degree angle—this achieves the best speed. As you come about and the bow of the boat is into the wind, the sails go slack, you release the sheets (ropes) holding the sails taunt. You quickly switch sides of the boat before the wind catches the sail from the other side, cinching the sheets in the opposite cleats and take off like a rocket going the other direction.

It's a pretty standard maneuver and relatively easy to do—less so in high winds and at speed. Since I was manning the jib, I was crawling under the mainsail boom on the canvas tarp that was stretched between the twin hulls of the cat, switching sides so I could move the jib across the bow quickly and catch the wind as we came about. But something odd happened. In my mind's eye I can still see it like it was yesterday; it takes the mind a moment to decipher and fully realize what was wrong even though you know intuitively what is. I was on my belly under the boom and should have had to look around the mast to see the jib sail. Yet, I could see the jib sail fully. There was no mast.

The mast that the main sail is attached to is about twenty-eight feet tall and weighs around 100lbs, with sail and rigging maybe 150lbs. It attaches at the center point on a beam that the tarp is attached to, running between the parallel hulls of the boat. There is a locking joint with a pin that allows it to swivel, and a cotter pin that keeps the pin from sliding out. Somewhere along our sail, the cotter pin sheared off. When slack came to the main sail, the pressure released on the pin and, because the mast is connected to the sides of the boat via stays (cables that keep the mast from ripping free from the hull when it lurches from side to side), the bottom of it kicked out in front of the boat. From my vantage, it simply was not there. And it should have been!

Time froze. There was no warning from my dad. Not sure he saw what was happening, or realized it, or was reflexively dodging out of the way at the same time as the mast came down but as I looked up, the mast that is usually perpendicular to the boat was now parallel and dropping straight towards me. I rolled left onto my back as it crashed onto the boat, taking the sails and stays with it and crushing the rudder handle that is used for steering, rendering the vessel dead in the water. Stupid Hobie Cat.

"Two passengers set sail that day for a one-hour tour, a one-hour tour…"

After the collective sigh of relief, no one was crushed under the mast, we took stock of our situation. We were the only boat on the

Gulf *brave* enough to sail in these conditions (all rentals had been put up) and were about a mile and a half from shore in high seas and with the mast and sail lying flat across the boat; that meant, we could not be seen from shore. Hmmm. But we did have our chaser.

Jim was idling about on the jet-ski, shaking his head. But he had power. By the time we had everything hooked up, and the rigging secured, since we had just made the channel when the mast came down, with the strong outward current we had drifted a little over two miles out. So, we took the main sheet and tied it to the back of the jet-ski and started the long tow towards shore.

"The weather started getting rough, the tiny ship was tossed..."

Jim was doing a pretty good job towing us. But with the rough seas, he really had to gun it to get the dead-weight boat up a swell, then as the boat came down the other side, it would quickly gain on him, so he'd have to throttle hard to keep from being overrun on the way down. This went on for about a half hour, until the Hobie overcame the jet ski on a particularly deep swell and the sheet line sucked into the prop on the back of the jet-ski...that was not good. The screw on a jet ski turns really fast to propel it upwards of fifty miles per hour, which meant that rope was wound really tight.

We couldn't pull it out, but maybe if we reached up into the out-take, we could loosen it. This was a job for Jim—as chaser. He made sure the engine was off and reached up in to start the long battle unwinding the rope. The battle lasted about a minute before he was cut pretty good on the extremely sharp blades of the screw. The jet-ski wasn't starting again. We took the jib sheet and tied the jet-ski to the Hobie, and both drifted...and drifted. The sun wasn't low in the sky yet, but it had dropped a little closer to the horizon and it wasn't getting warmer.

41

Luckily—actually, there was no luck about it, the base team (family) on the beach had seen the sail disappear. So had the Marine Patrol, the Coast Guard, and about ten other good citizens, who called 911. The Marine Patrol reached us first. They said they had received several calls and triangulated our drift with the Coast Guard from where we were last seen and had made a beeline straight to us. By now the temperature was dropping, but because we were unhurt, they could not take us aboard—we had to stay on the Hobie.

Except Jim. He was smart enough to get cut when he stuck his hand up in the jet-ski, so he got on-board, due to an injury, and sat in the warm cabin drinking fresh cocoa. Bugger. The Marines stayed with us until a salvage ship they'd called arrived to tow us in. Jim went back to shore with the Marine Patrol.

> *"If not for the courage of the fearless crew, the Hobie*
> *would be lost.*
> *The Hobie would be lost…"*

It was a slow drag. Because of the rough seas, they could only tow us at about one half-knot per hour (0.57 mph). If you do the math, two miles out equals about three and a half hours. And as it got cooler, with nothing but wet T-shirts and board shorts, as the ocean spray misted over us at every wave, we were freezing.

Back on dry land, the base team was pacing frantically, and strictly for medicinal purposes, drinking copious amounts of wine, but had received word from the Marine Patrol that there was a bead on us, and a salvage company had been called to bring us to the bay boat ramps for exfiltration—all they needed was a credit card. The salvage company had to ask a second time if the base had heard that payment was required, or we'd be set back adrift. After an uncomfortably long pause, the base team reluctantly agreed to pay.

By the time we were towed through the channel and into the bay where the boat ramps were, the sun had set, and it was considerably cooler than when our adventure started some five hours earlier. Our fingers were frozen around the gear we were holding in place and our lips were blue, but we'd made it to dry land. Brother Tim had to literally help pry my fingers loose from the rigging. Jim was comfortably warm by now and he, Tim, and Keith put the boat away while my dad and I thawed out in the car.

> *"So, this is the tale of our sailing team,*
> *They were out for a long, long time.*
> *They had to make up with their wives,*
> *T'was an uphill climb. T'was an uphill climb."*

That ended the trip for the Hobie cat, but she would sail again many times. Until hurricane Ivan took her away forever along with sand dunes in '04. Now she lives on in the Eigel clan's hearts and these tales of yore.

The Ballad of Gilligan's Island —mostly
[Recorded 1964 ~ Sherwood Schwartz and George Wyle]

The Hobie Cat in Her Glory Days ~ Panama City Beach, 1996

—Chapter Eight—

Shotgun Stealth in Tighty-Whities—1997

The Eigel Boys Gang ~ circa 1978

It was 1978. A new car was about $5,000 and a gallon of gas was sixty-five cents. It was the era of mood rings, bell-bottom pants and big hair. Star Wars had swept the nation and Sally Ride was the first woman astronaut.

Back when I was young, guns were not the hot topic of controversy they are today. My father was an avid hunter and had an assortment of shotguns, rifles, and pistols. The rifles and shotguns were displayed in an open gunrack in the family room and all four of us boys understood they were not toys and were taught to respect them — and not to touch them for fear of being knocked upside the head with the butt of one of those things.

I loved watching westerns on TV with my dad. It was great time spent with him and he imparted knowledge of what kinds of guns were being used and whether real cowboys could shoot like they did in the movies. "Yes," he would say, "John Wayne could, in fact, shoot a single-action Colt .45 pistol in one hand, a Winchester 1892 saddle ring carbine in the other, spin-cocking and shooting it one-handed with horse reins in his teeth." Everyone knew that. It was legend!

We didn't have a lot of games growing up, certainly no video games — they didn't even really exist. Pong had barely been on the market, and it could not hold our attention long. Pong was the first home video game, it was black and white, with two single-knob controllers. It was essentially two-dimensional table tennis or "ping-pong," played on the TV. It held our attention all of four minutes.

With little else to do, we improvised and either played cowboys and Indians, or army, or cops and robbers — all with toy guns. We had to concoct our attire from our standard wardrobes, and therefore didn't really have too many authentic-looking outfits. Hence, the 1978 picture above, which was a combination of western flare with, in my case, a Han Solo influence. Tim went for the Starsky and Hutch look and Jim took my cue, unbuttoning his shirt three or four buttons. Chest hair was a long way off, but we looked svelte. At least for seven, ten, and thirteen-year-olds, we thought we did.

Since we didn't have leather holsters, we were forced to use our colored baseball belts, which would stretch tight enough to stay in place and still hold our weapons. If we were looking to blend, to melt into the setting, to become one with our environment, well, not sure we really accomplished that—unless we were undercover in a department store's clearance section. But we could strike a gunslinger pose flawlessly—and we looked tough as hell. Never mind the fact that we had to have our mom take our picture in the family room.

Personally, I wore my gun-belt low across my hip, so I could quick-draw if a confrontation sprang up. Brother Tim used the tried and true thigh-belt-holster, which actually was a favorite of undercover female cops. His gun-belt always matched the sleeves on his jacket too; very stylish. Young James wore his gun-belt more as an accessory, going with the high-waisted cross-draw setup, but since he was touting a sawed-off submachine gun, it wasn't too functional for holstering his weapon anyhow.

You might wonder why two of the Eigel Boy Gang members were in socks. It wasn't because we were in stealth mode to sneak up on the bad guys. No, it was because our shoes were dirty, and we'd get in real trouble if we tracked dirt through the house.

Even with all of our playing guns, I didn't really learn all that much about them back in the day. You would think I would have, with my dad being an expert marksman, a champion skeet shooter and avid hunter. But see, when I really hit those formative years, Star Wars came out and everything was all about lasers and blasters. The guns of the future.

Fast forward about twenty years to 1997. I was now thirty-two years old and married with two kids of my own. We had just moved into a new house and were settling in, but hadn't figured out all the nuances. One of those was the alarm system. It was fancier than we were used to — we were used to a dog barking, a shotgun, and a landline to call 911 if there was a break-in. This newfangled system had motion detectors, window sensors, zones, the works. Very state-of-the-art.

So, one night about 2:00 a.m., the alarm goes off. High-pitched whistles screeching, my wife, Maureen and I bolted upright! I jumped out of that bed like I had been ejected from a cockpit, landing deftly in the crouching-tiger pose, all senses on high-alert. It was still dark in the room and, after a few moments, Maureen turned on the bedside lamp to reveal I had shifted subconsciously to the Karate Kid stork-pose, standing on one-foot, other leg high in the air in front of me, hands extended outward from my sides — in my underwear. Tighty-whities. No t-shirt, just the briefs. That is not so attractive a look now, but twenty years ago I was a little more buff (30 lbs. lighter) and in my defense, boxer-briefs hadn't taken hold yet. No pun intended.

Remembering my training from my youth, and with children and a wife to protect, I grabbed my short-barrel shotgun and readied to head into danger. Maureen had determined that we had a motion sensor tripped in the basement, but no door or windows had been breached. By now the alarm company had called and Maureen was on the phone giving them a SITREP. (Situational Report for non-military folk)

I cocked the gun and headed from the upstairs down to the main level. On tip-toes, I quietly made my way through the main floor to the basement staircase. My heart was thundering in my ears, perspiration starting to bead at my hairline. I couldn't hear anything or see anything since the staircase to the basement took a forty-five degree turn halfway to the bottom. As I crept downward, I remembered Bradly (a friend of the family who knows all things guns, military and defense) saying something about if an intruder was in the house, just the sound of a shotgun cocking was enough to make them flee. It is indeed a terrifying sound if you're not the one holding the gun.

So, I cocked the shotgun. Again. Yep, when you do that a second time, the chambered shell ejects as the new one goes in. With my particular shotgun, it ejects from a port on the righthand side of the gun. In the tight stairwell, it bounced off the wall and before I could duck, hit me in the side of the head, then clattered to the floor. As I stood there in my underwear. It wasn't funny.

No one charged me while I reeled from my miscue. No one bolted from the basement. No one was there at all. Not even a mouse. Which is what we later surmised had set off the alarm in the first place. That or my son Jack's missing hamster, whose carcass was found years later. Both relieved and dejected, I made my way back upstairs with the shotgun over my shoulder and gave Maureen the all-clear and she gave the safe code to the alarm company. I was starting to catch a chill, so I put the gun away and climbed back in bed, ending our (un)eventful night. Stupid shotgun shell.

Very glad we didn't have cellphone cameras back then.

"Do not go where the path may lead, go instead where there is no path and leave a trail."
[Ralph Waldo Emerson ~ 1803–1882 ~ American Poet]

—Chapter Nine—

I'm a Handful—2001

Classic Maddie Meltdown ~ 1999 Grandparents 50th

S ometimes you just have to laugh—or else you might commit unspeakable crimes. No, not really, but maybe. Back in our early parenting days, we ran smack-dab into the terrible twos and they lasted a good bit longer than the second year. Our own adorable daughter, acting on her own volition, inadvertently discouraged friends and family not only from wanting children of their own but also from even trying to conceive. But I get ahead of myself; let me set the scene.

We had our second child in 1996, and she was absolutely beautiful. Well, not right at first—even though everyone says how beautiful newborns are, they can really be quite ugly. Everyone thinks their own baby is God's gift to the world—and many may turn out to be, but right at first, if we're being totally honest: they are not attractive little humans. They are not like cute little puppies or panda bears. But Madison turned out to be beautiful, and near perfect. She giggled when you changed her. She went to bed without a fuss. Ate whatever she was served. Always made us smile. This little angel was *beyond*.

We had heard about the terrible twos and thought we were prepared to handle them when they arrived. But having not experienced them with our firstborn, who was then almost 7, how bad could they be? Madison had always been an early learner, whether it's because she loved her older brother and wanted to follow in his footsteps, or whether she just had the drive, I don't know, but she seemed always ahead of the curve. Thus, the terrible twos came for us at about fourteen months. And, as Madison always gave 110% and was a perfectionist, she perfected them for almost three years before finally growing out of them.

Oh, the stories of Maddie Meltdowns—known far and wide in the Northern Atlanta area and still talked of in hushed tones in the Florida Pan Handle. The picture above was captured by the event photographer when she was three years old at her grandparent's fiftieth anniversary party. I'm not sure what the impetus of this specific meltdown was, but it was epic. It stopped the dancing. Stopped the band. Stopped the entire party, as you can see her grandmother and me trying to talk sense to her, to little effect; her brother Jack's expression says it all: seen this before. It's not going to end well. Move along.

We lived on a cul-de-sac and one day our neighbor Colleen, who lived four houses up the street, called Maureen to tell her that she could hear Madison screaming from inside her house and did she know she was out in the front yard. Maureen said *yes*, she knew Madison was in the front yard screaming; that was where she had left her.

There was one family trip to Panama City Beach with the extended Eigel family, including my Aunts and Uncles, et al. We had meltdowns in the condo. On the beach. A classic highchair bang-rocking tantrum in Captain Anderson's Seafood Restaurant. If we were writing a Dr. Seuss book, it would go on for pages—she had a meltdown on a train. On a plane. In the car. At the bar. Here and there. She had meltdowns everywhere. You get the gist. Hysterical or at least amusing to look back on now, but to live them—Oi vey. And I'm not even Jewish.

The year she turned five, we were visiting one of her aunt and uncle's, it was the summer of 2001. By that time, the meltdowns were well behind us and she had become a Barbie doll aficionado, having progressed unscathed from the Teletubby years—if you don't know what Teletubbies are, count your blessings and look for my upcoming story "She was a Po child born in Hickory Flat, Georgia."

As you do with little kids, her uncle asked her to tell him how old she was. As she ticked off her fingers—half to herself, counting off one at a time and ending with an outstretched palm, she looked up and said, "I'm a handful." If that response didn't encapsulate the first five years of her life perfectly, I'm not sure what would.

Madison at age 5 ~ the summer of 2001

We may have had lots of angst in those dark days, and probably have a few telltale tics if a child within earshot screams at the right pitch, but Madison quickly grew out of her meltdowns and once again became perfection. I think she compressed a lifetime of past and future dark moments into those two years, ten months and seventeen days. But she really has been a ray of sunshine for our family ever since.

From then on, she has always been the one filled with unabashed laughter, often at my expense, but even that's okay! Her sense of humor is well honed and to this day, at twenty-years old, she still has that infectious laugh and brightens any room. I would take those couple years of meltdowns to get the next seventeen years of joy and determination with nary a second thought. I defy anyone to meet a more gregarious and charming soul.

"To me there is no picture so beautiful as smiling, bright-eyed, happy children; no music so sweet as their clear and ringing laughter."
[P.T. Barnum ~ 1810–1891 ~ American Entertainer]

—Chapter Ten—

Ol' Smokey—2001

Smokey and Dad napping –circa 2001

H ave you ever had that pet that was just amazing, but whose
time was drawing near? Whether a cat or dog, or even a
fish… well, not really a fish. Fish don't fetch the paper or nuzzle
up and lay on your feet. They stare at you, if you're lucky, for a
few moments and then swim the other way with no memory of you
from that moment before. Can't really say fish are amazing pets.
They might be for your cat, if you own a cat. I'm not as big on

cats. Cats have attitude and they do not give unfettered love—at least not to me.

I know some cat owners, and they're a little crazy. Like their cats. Have I got a cat story—not for cat lovers and for another time; this story is about a dog. Dog owners can be crazy too, but mostly I've found dog owners are both empathetic and resolute at the same time—which makes them dogmatic regarding dogs. Which is ironic.

This story is about our dog Smokey. Smokey was given to us by my brother, who was moving and had no real yard for the dog in a new house, had little kids, and couldn't focus on the dog to care for it properly. My wife Maureen cares for every dog properly. She cares for her dogs—yes, plural; we have had many and usually two or more at a time. She cares for her dogs more than she cares for me. If life is reincarnated, I have to come back as one of her dogs. It would be only fair, since I have missed out on this devoted love and affection since we've owned dogs, which has been longer than our thirty years of marriage. Additionally, I am quite familiar with the doghouse.

So, we took on Smokey as our third dog. Smokey was incredible. A big black lab with brown eyes that would melt the coldest of hearts. Smokey was smart and well trained, too. My father raised hunting dogs when he was young and could train them to do amazing things—not stupid, cute things like shake and rollover. Have you ever had a guest over in a white dress whom bends down to say "hi" to your dog that has been taught to shake, but has muddy paws? Smokey was the best-trained dog we ever owned. She would fetch, but not until you told her it was okay to fetch. When told to heel, she would circle you once and sit. She would "speak" when you wiggled your little finger. And the all-important stay; she would actually stay when you told her to.

Smokey was the perfect balance of loving and protective.

She was a little like Dug in the movie Up—although our dialog was unspoken, it was there.

"You are my master and I will love you
Go away Smokey.
I will go away and I will still love you.
Lie down!
I will lie down after I tell you one more time I love you, by licking your face.
Stay
I will stay now and will still love you."

She was protective of both Maureen and our kids. But a child could pull on her ears, step on her tail, try to ride her like a miniature horse, which my son tried many times, and she never growled or snapped. She was amazing. We didn't have her for her whole life, but for seven or eight good years. By the time she turned thirteen, she was on Rimadyl for arthritis (hip dysplasia is typical in older labs) and steadily going downhill.

Eventually, it was clear that she was headed for the dirt nap, when she couldn't get herself up, wasn't eating, and was clearly in pain and suffering. I had taken our previous dog to the vet to be put down a few years prior and wasn't going to go through that again. I know it's the humane thing to do but, being handed the collar after a dog is put to sleep is about as unpleasant an experience as I can recall. We didn't know how else to send her on her way (now that we were living in a neighborhood with firearm discharge restrictions—not that I could have really done that anyway). So, Maureen said she would take her.

We (by "we," I mean Maureen) agreed it was time, and one Saturday morning we put blankets in the back of the car, and I carried old Smokey out and put her in the back. We said our tearful goodbyes and Maureen drove off. The kids were dejected, and the neighbors gathered in our front yard when they saw what was going on. We lived on a cul-de-sac then and most of the neighbors were a pretty tight group of friends; one of them who moved away fifteen years ago, but are still as good of friends as though they are still living next door, said that group of neighbors was like catching lightning in a bottle—which is about right.

Maureen had been gone awhile and as we hung out waiting for her to return, we were trying to decide if everyone should be in the yard when she came back. Or if she would rather have time to herself, as Maureen is a fairly private person. Since I'm just her husband, I wasn't sure what the right thing to do was.

About then, her car turned down the street and it would have been odd for the neighbors to scatter and hide, since she could see us standing in the front yard. With heavy hearts, we watched Maureen get out of the car. I expected tears, or maybe at least remnants of them. But she didn't look upset. I thought, man, she's handling this well—certainly better than I did...what the hell? Was she tougher than me?

We all stood silent in that awkward moment of not knowing what to say. She looked over furtively at the throng standing there as she got out and opened the back door from which bounded a rejuvenated Smokey—who loped around the yard, rolled over, scratched her back on the lawn, saw a "squirrel!" and took off on the chase. What?

The group of us was dumbstruck, and Maureen was grinning like the Cheshire cat. How was this even possible? It was a miracle—a $300 shot in the butt miracle. The vet gave her a shot and she was good to go. She wasn't done yet! So, we got ol' Smokey back and she lived for at least another $4000.

Got to love a happy ending!

"Second star to the right, and straight on 'til morning..."
[Peter Pan ~ 1953 ~ Disney Character]

—Chapter Eleven—

Smokey the Sequel—2002

Madison Marie unbridled ~ circa 2002

When my daughter, Maddie, was little she had a very active imagination. She played with all sorts of stuffed animals and dolls for which she created identities, complete with backstories and probably biographies. She and one of her childhood girlfriends still laugh, albeit haltingly, about being able to sit and play for hours with erasers where they conjured up interactions and personalities that went with them. They were little people-shaped erasers, but still, come-on, who spends time coming up with all that instead of just playing with already formed dolls that were more resembling people?

She would play for hours. She was one of those who was more interested in utilizing the box a toy came in than the actual toy. Well—unless it was a stuffed toy, then it was hugged and giggled at the second it was free of its trappings. "It's so soft and fluffy!" But you get the gist, creative, right-brain all the way.

Over the years, Maddie has accumulated many dolls and Barbies and stuffed animals from soft and cute to those disgusting "ugly dolls," and everything in between. However, this story takes place when she was six-years old. Her artistic ingenuity was manifesting itself with all sorts of lame toys that came to life in great and tragic tales.

We had a pretty big section of our basement unfinished back then, and the dogs would go in and out of the house this way through a doggie door. It was big enough for a 100 lb. Lab to fit through, but still a "doggie" door to us. We had games setup in the basement— actually had a fast-rolling bocce court and, like everybody with a basement, we stored boxes and other useless junk—some of it moved from our previous houses unopened.

For a box-loving, creative kid with a spirited inventiveness, the unfinished basement was perfect. Except, she had to share it with the stupid dogs. They would wander through her setups, generally knocking over dolls or, heaven forbid, pickup one in their mouth. In either case, tears were usually the result and the dogs called very inspired names.

But the tears would dry, usually an ice-cream sandwich or cookies would dry them up, and the dogs would be scolded, but since my wife is a dog lover, they too would be given a treat. Maddie had this large doll house with her family of people, including extended family and friends with their own little plastic cars and tables and beds and probably dishes too. A complete dollhouse—one she played with for long spans of time.

In the previous chapter about Smokey the dog, at thirteen and near what we thought was the end, she came back, almost literally from the dead, from a shot in the haunches that gave her new life. And while we enjoyed ol' Smokey through the next year, there were periods when she did lose control of some functionality and continence from time to time.

This made the basement situation even more precarious, so Maddie built up walls with cardboard and boxes to keep the dogs out. In today's vernacular, it would have been designated a safe space or sanctuary city.

There were several occasions that year where the dog would leave unwanted presents that would have to be cleaned up, before play could continue and all Maddie's dolls, cars, little doll dogs, and all elements would have to be inspected for collateral damage, etc. You get the picture. Lots of soap and water, (I don't think hand sanitizer had been invented yet, and if it had we should have bought stock), was used in those days and something the "parents" were responsible for, since Maddie did not want to share space with dogs. In our defense, the dogs acted on their own recognizance.

One unfortunate day, while Maddie was out attending to other matters, Ol' Smokey could not make it outside in a timely manner, and not wanting to do business where she ate, made her way unabated into the sanctuary city, and carpet bombed. From the perspective of six-inch tall dolls, this was a massive overkill—shock and awe, if you will.

My wife, Maureen, discovered the carnage and, while it could have been way more horrific than it was, didn't have time to cleanup before Maddie returned from whatever excursion she was on. Maureen reported the accident to Maddie to ready her, before she went downstairs. Maddie paled and, swallowing hard, inquired as to which dolls were hit. Delicately, Maureen explained the Daddy doll was hit solidly. Only the Daddy doll? Yes, just the Daddy doll.

Have you ever heard the unbridled, hysterical, unending laughter of children? It is in fact intoxicating and infectious, but surely can be irreverent as well. Maddie is twenty-two now and when we recount this tale she laughs as hard as she did when she was six-years old all over again. It's never funnier than when dear old dad is the butt of a good narrative—literally.

In and of itself, this story is not all that funny, but that response was absolutely hilarious to us, and revealed at a very not-so-tender-as-it-turns-out age, just a little insight into my sweet daughter's absolute love for deprecating slapstick.

"Laughter is timeless. Imagination has no age.
And dreams are forever."
[Walt Disney ~ 1901–1966 ~ American Entrepreneur]

—Chapter Twelve—

Life's Lessons in Sports—2004

State Champions ~ circa 2004

J ust after the turn of the century, our children were young, and our lives were crazy. Many of us parents have experienced those years, where just catching a day off from family activities is like an entire week at the spa. I was doing everything. And my wife, Maureen was, without a doubt, the glue that held it all together. But this little account is about how teenagers can be awful, which we all know, and how they can be wonderful, which fewer of us know.

I had sold my company the year prior and was working as a VP in Business Development, so had flex in my schedule—which I needed. I was commissioner of a twenty-team softball league, I was running our neighborhood bowling league, captain of my tennis team, on the neighborhood homeowners board, coaching both kids' soccer teams, and Jack's roller hockey team at the same time; you get the idea. The only day of the week open was Friday. Maureen was not sufficiently attended to that year.

My son Jack had turned thirteen in April of 2004. And for six months, it was like someone had taken a giant eyedropper of "asshole" and squeezed it out on his head. It was truly bizarre, until he was twelve, he was all boy for sure, but a great kid. And about mid-fall he got back to being a great kid, but in between he knew everything and I was an idiot, out of touch, scruffy looking, a bad father and a terrible coach—who's scruffy looking?

Amidst all of that, a good friend of mine, Bob Chapin, and I combined our boy's rec-league soccer teams. We had been rivals on the field for years, but as the boys got older and other sports took precedence over recreational soccer, we pooled our two teams with the kids still in the program. This might have been the best thing we ever did, because these were the kids who chose soccer and we were able to hold the team together for two years. And we brought home the hardware. Two State Championships.

But the funny thing is, it was never about the hardware. That just happened. The stories within those two seasons are some of my fondest. Coaching boys was both trying and exhilarating. They were all about playing, learning, conditioning, and testosterone.

They wanted to be there. Contrast that with coaching girls—holy parallel universe Batman! Girls were about social, having fun, and not sweating. And when they were older, about the boys.

A few years later, as my daughter Maddie got older, and I was coaching sixteen some-odd thirteen and fourteen-year-old girls; it was way harder than anything I went through with the boys. I had to have that talk with them, about if they weren't feeling well, then they had to tell me, before I had to pull them out of the game for standing still and crying. If you know me, it was harder to give that little speech than to say my wedding vows.

Boys I could relate to; between Bob and me we discovered some great coaching tactics and motivational techniques that worked incredibly well. At one particular practice, I arrived about forty minutes late and Bob was sitting in a folding chair reading the paper. The boys were still running laps. I asked Bob what the plan was for practice and he said, "This is it." They were goofing off during warm-ups, were being totally obstinate and disrespectful, so the entire practice they ran laps. That was a Tuesday night. The next practice, two nights later, was the best practice we ever had. And from then on, all we had to do was pull a paper out and snap it open and they fell immediately in line, doing whatever we asked with renewed zeal.

Another tactic that paid dividends a hundred times over, I have relayed to every coach I have met since. We were struggling with how to effectively discipline one of our good defensive players, Jared. He was garnering attention from the other boys and con-stantly acting out. He would slap down the ball with his hand, and we'd make him run a lap, for those of you that don't know, you're not allowed to touch the ball with your hands in soccer unless you're the goalie/keeper. But our discipline wasn't having any affect, because he was still getting props from the other boys even though he was in trouble. Then Bob had a great idea.

The next time he slapped down the ball with his hand in the middle of play, we stopped practice. He was getting ready to run when we said, "Oh no. Jared, you stand here, and the entire team will take a lap for you until you can learn to control yourself." You should have seen the wave of dread come across his face and halfway around the field you could hear his teammates loud and clear: "Jared, you suck!" "Come on Jared!" He never did it again. In fact, no one on the team did. Jared became one of our best players, with the most positive attitude you could hope for.

But the best coaching didn't come from Bob or me. We were in a no-cut Rec league, so anyone who signed up, made the team. And every player had to play a minimum of half the game. We had one particular player on the team, who was not as athletic as most of the boys, who could not run as fast, or control the ball as well. And the other boys picked on him and teased him.

Finally, I had had enough. I pulled the three leaders on the team aside and told them that we were likely headed toward winning the league. But the constant berating wasn't helping the team. We had to play all players half the game and we were only as strong as our weakest link. They needed to encourage and help the weaker players so the whole team would be stronger, or our opponents would find those weaknesses and exploit them.

So, slowly but steadily, the compliments started coming in. When he wouldn't do something right, one of the better boys would take him aside and encourage him. As this happened, confidence grew. As confidence grew, so did skills and, as skills grew, the other boys were motivated to help him, all the more. By the time we were in the State Championship game, he wasn't our strongest player, but there wasn't anyone else on the field with more heart in the game. The best coaching had come from his peers. And they rooted for him with gusto!

At one point in the game, he had been run over and was bleeding from a pretty good scrape on his knee. At the beginning of the season, he would have begged to come out of the game. He put his bent glasses back on, brushed the grass off his face, and refused to be pulled out, playing with twice the determination. We would end up tying in regulation play that final game. In the second over-time, we had a crossing pass from our left forward to our striker, right in front of the goal, who won the championship game with a header! It was as dramatic a finish to an incredible season as you could conceivably hope for. One that makes you proud to just have been there.

Bob and I call those our greatest years coaching. But it wasn't just us. The right mix of kids with the right attitudes and anything is possible. I'll take a team full of hustlers, over a team full of talent every single time. Win or lose, those are the stories I really value.

"Sports do not build character. They reveal it."
[Heywood Braun ~ 1888–1939 ~ American Journalist]

Chapter Thirteen

How do Dogs Know? — 2005

Riley before she became a ...dog. ~ circa 2004

There are only so many trophies that you truly earn in life. When I was growing up, there were first and second place trophies, maybe a third, if you were in a big enough league of some kind, but none of these namby-pamby participation trophies that kids get nowadays. When I played baseball there may have been an MVP trophy—which I would have said was pretty awesome, but I never earned it, so I classify it as useless.

In fact, when I was coaching my son at the YMCA when he was seven or eight, halfway through our first game, I asked the Ref, since the scoreboard apparently was broken, who was keeping track of the score? I was told that, at the Y, there were no winners and losers, they're all winners and they didn't keep score; it was turned off. I said *bullshit*. I didn't say it in front of the kids, although that would have been a good lesson for them to learn; how Refs aren't always right.

No; part of learning any sport completely, is learning how to be both a good winner and a good loser, and the only way to teach that is to experience it. So, every team we played, I would talk to the other coach before the game and, without fail, they all agreed that we would keep our own scores and we taught the kids how to win and lose. We didn't win many games, but our kids learned what it meant to lose and that as you go through life there are winners and losers. Once you're out of school and in the grown-up world, you need to know how to deal with both.

Our team was not the worst that year—but close. When the league gave me the participation trophies, I never handed them out.

Fast forward another ten years and one of the things you earn when you win your division, in tennis, is a bag tag. Coveted bling amongst the weekend warriors, albeit plastic bling. You collect a few of these babies and when you walk on the court, the opponents know you've got game—or at the least were on a team that had game. I had collected several of these bag tags over the years and kept them on the outside of the bag so they would clickety-clack if you swung your hips just right. Intimidate the hell out of the opponent. Maybe. Not really, but still, they were coveted. By me.

74

Our dog was a one-year-old puppy at the time. Cute little dog named Riley. My son, Jack, and his Mom rescued her at the Humane Society. That is a whole 'nother story! We had always had big Labs or Goldens and Riley is about a 40 lb. mix between a Standard and Spitz. She was cute as could be as a puppy, but as she grew didn't play well with other dogs and is the definition of an Alpha. The kids loved Riley though and if you know Maureen, you know that no dog of hers goes unloved. If I come back as anything, I wouldn't be president, I wouldn't be a rock star or a millionaire, I wouldn't be human at all—I'd be one of Maureen's dogs. That is the life.

Riley and I didn't really see eye-to-eye in those days. If I'm being honest, we never did, but it was hard not to give her scraps from the table and secretly I had a soft spot for her (don't tell anyone!). But we had history—her chewing the wiring harness on my John Deere that led to her flying lesson, chewing my slippers, peeing at the base of my chair in the family room. Crapping in the front yard. Burning holes in the lawn with her acrid urine. The list goes on and on.

The family was going to be gone for a long weekend, and we had one of the neighbor kids let Riley out and feed her while we were gone. We debated boarding her, but she was young and was becoming better behaved. So, we decided we didn't have too much stuff she could chew up and really ruin and decided to risk leaving her. We set her up with all her dog toys, the squeakers had been ripped out of any that had them within moments of receiving them, and she had all kinds of things to play with in our absence.

We came home—not without some trepidation but trusting she would not have caused major damage. We checked everywhere and could find nothing amiss. No messes. No piles or puddles. No chewed chair or table legs. Nada. She was the perfect canine.

Surprising for sure; I was impressed because I naturally assumed the worst and Maureen got her once-in-a-lifetime "I told you so" chit. I was glad to give it—It wasn't really her only chit, I've had to give them countless times, usually not for dogs doing what they were supposed to, however.

Then came the next Saturday morning. I kept my tennis bag in a closet in my home-office and went to grab it for the match I was playing that morning. I had about eight or ten bag tags on the bag, including the one from the previous season. It was still in the plastic wrapper, inside the bag. That was the one thing she chewed up! She had left all the tags, and the bag, and the racquets, and balls, and old sweatbands, free of destruction. The one thing she must have known meant the most in that assortment, was the most recent bag tag, which would show opponents that I was a current force to be reckoned with.

She somehow got into a closed closet, into the tennis bag, nosed through the compartments and took the bag tag out of the bag, out of the sealed wrapper and chewed it mercilessly. Then closed the door behind her. How in high hell did she know to pull out that one bag tag, out of my tennis bag, which was still in the plastic, and chew it up?

The puppy was smart, I guess. Maureen said so before and certainly at that moment it was confirmed for her. And she took Riley's side! Something along the lines of, "You should have been nicer to her. She knows what you like. See how karma bites you." *Bite* was the correct turn of phrase. I think Riley did it to spite me and I told her very sternly it was a huge black mark in my doggie score-book. Pretty sure that never bothered her though. Our relationship eventually healed, but it was never the same.

If they weren't so stinking cute when they're little.

"It's not the size of the dog in the fight;
it's the size of the fight in the dog."
[Mark Twain ~ 1835–1910 ~ American Author]

—Chapter Fourteen—

Wrong Car, Sir—2006

Our sweet little yellow X-terra shamed by a gas-guzzling shiny new yellow Hummer H2. I would love to own the H2…

It was spring of 2006, a chance to spend the evening away at a nice restaurant. The kids were with Grandma, so we could enjoy a night out. My wife, Maureen, and I went down to a local steak joint in the city. We weren't exactly flush with cash but, splurging for our anniversary was something we could justify. We'd saved money in other ways, taking ~~fewer~~ no vacation trips, not decorating ~~every~~ any room in the house, not driving an expensive car.

Actually, the car was a bit of a sore spot—it was purchased used and, while it was great for lugging the kids around, it was perhaps not my best automotive buy, in my storied career of car buying. It was a bright yellow Nissan Xterra SUV with a sports luggage rack on top. It looked like a taxicab to be sure, but when you parked in a crowded parking lot (coming out of the mall for example), you could, without fail, spot it immediately.

When I bought it, I was told there only eleven in the city, and I believed it because who would buy so boldly; although it did seem popular with my Latin American brethren. Funny thing though, those eleven other owners must have lived on the north side of the city somewhere near us and were on my same schedule, because over the months and years that followed the purchase, there sure were a lot on the road when I was.

We enjoyed the dinner; perfectly cooked steaks and some fine wine. We talked about life and children, family and friends, good times and bad. A rare date night that was uninterrupted and quiet. The conversation eventually circled around to the car and we laughed about how it was not quite as fancy as others that were valeting when we pulled up, and how the twenty-somethings were likely fighting over who got to drive it.

See, I had traded in my black, five-speed Mustang convertible that shook your pant legs when it idled if you wandered in too close. It was a sweet little muscle car that you could throttle down and turn every male head, and several female ones as well, as you rumbled through the neighborhood. Huh-hu-huh! But I had a tough choice to make. I was coaching two kids in three sports and, with the Mustang, it had a really small back seat. I could only fit so many bags of soccer balls, different sizes for the two kids, and hockey equipment AND the kids.

I did have options: I could leave one kid at the curb and fit the equipment in the back seat and trunk, go home and come back and get the left-over kid, which to be fair, I would have rotated turns so neither one felt singled out—even though Maddie was only ten and Jack was about to turn fifteen. Or I could take both kids and some of the equipment, leave some of the equipment, go home and come back and get the left-over equipment. In either case, it was dicey whether whatever or whomever I left behind would be there when I got back. Since Maureen said a coin toss was not a solution, we sold the Mustang and went car hunting. And came home with the yellow Xterra.

Back to the dinner. Once we paid the check, we strolled back towards the valet; it had gotten considerably busier. The young guys were really hoofing it and doing a pretty good job from my perspective. A crowd of folks had formed, who were in the process of dropping a car, or picking one up, or waiting on theirs to be brought around. We handed our stub to the valet and edged to the back of the pack.

While we were waiting, we (meaning me) may have made a few wine-induced snarky comments about the Mercedes and Jaguars, setting-up for a payoff line when they brought ours around. But then they brought the car around really fast. In my demure fashion and in an effort to laugh away our conspicuously inferior ride, with a little self-deprecating humor, I belt out, "That is a sweet ride! The Valet must have parked that baby in a prime spot to bring it around so fast!" It garnered a few smiles and maybe a chuckle or two. I think I heard a chuckle.

I pushed Maureen past two women who were starting forward; she hops in the passenger side as I climb in the driver side while handing over my two-dollar tip and the valet looking perplexed says, "Excuse me sir, this isn't the right ticket." About the same time, Maureen is noticing there is something not quite familiar inside the car and I am catching out of the corner of my eye a second yellow Nissan Xterra with the same luggage rack about four cars back. "Uh, Maureen, this isn't our car."

I did apologize, over Maureen's gales of laughter, for being an ass; that's what the two women whose car it actually was, called me. We didn't really garner too many sympathetic looks from the crowd either, especially after my build-up to deliver the one-liner that really fell flat after pushing two women out of the way to get in their car. They didn't really appreciate my explanation of feigned grandiose, and wasn't it funnier now that they could see we had the exact same car? No. It wasn't. So, we surreptitiously slunk back to the line and waited for the other yellow Nissan Xterra. This time I tipped five dollars.

"There is a thin line that separates laughter and pain, comedy and tragedy, humor and hurt."
[Erma Bombeck ~ 1927–1996 ~ American Journalist]

—Chapter Fifteen—

Nightmare at 20 Feet—2008

William Shatner in "The Twilight Zone" ~ © 1963

T he day started off innocently enough. It would soon spiral. Flying can always be a challenge, but when you're not a Medallion flyer, there is little hope of avoiding the middle seat, the odiferous passenger, the halitosis chatterer, or the dreaded fleshy flyer. Yes, long before I logged enough miles to earn that Medallion status, where upgrades are more plentiful, Delta Comfort was an option or I had a choice of seats in an exit row or window/aisle, I too, was a passenger in what I refer to as steerage. You must minimize those precious minutes or hours when you are trapped in an aluminum tube with wings that hurtles through the atmosphere at 525 mph and 35,000 feet.

The whine of the Pitney-Bowes jet engines when they hit full thrust can barely be muffled by an expensive set of Bose Acoustical headphones—a must if you've got a Chatty Cathy, a crying baby or a snorer within earshot. The vibration is stronger in steerage as those engines throttle up and the landing can compress the strongest of spines, if your pilot happens to have landed fighters on aircraft carriers in his former life. Worse than all of that, is the lack of buffer arm-rests, unless you happen to have secured the coveted exit row seats, where the divider goes all the way down and someone's fat can't ooze under the armrest, encroaching on your sacred seat space that you've paid for the privilege of occupying.

This was one of those flights. No exit row, but at least a window. The plane was almost finished boarding for a 6:40 a.m. departure, the flight attendants announcing it was a completely full flight and please store only one item in the overhead bins and keep your second item under the seat in front of you. Great. There couldn't have been but a few seats left to fill when I saw her behind three skinny folks. A fleshy flyer. Large—very large—tank-top/muumuu, exposed fleshy arms. Oh, please God, let her pass. Let this cup pass. I mean that cup floweth way over.

But no, she was going to squeeze all 380 lbs. into that middle seat that's twenty-two inches wide, right between me and some other poor sap whose eyes were like saucers as the revelation hit him that she was sitting between us. Like a trained special-ops warrior, my defense mechanisms kicked in: in a split second, the sleeves were rolled down to avoid flesh-on-flesh, the arm rest was firmly seated in its lowest position to minimize the buttocks and thigh adipose encroachment—all I could do was gaze out the window and feign great interest in what the guy with the ear protection and those short, red lightsabers was doing. You could almost hear the sucking sound as her mass filled the space between the armrests. A giant round peg in a tiny square hole, if there ever was one.

My back now twisted and pressed against the window to give room, was not nearly enough to make way for her massive girth. There's no way this large woman didn't know the twenty to thirty percent of space the passenger to her right and, me, to her left, wasn't hers— and I'm no small fry at six-foot-two inches and 200+ lbs. To her credit, it's a very small credit, she tried to keep her stuff—purse, arms, some bonnet-looking head garb, her feedbag, in her "space." She folded her arms up on top of her massive bosom, which put her elbows and forearms about equal to the height of her chins. *Okay*, I thought, *she's trying to not encroach further than the laws of physics demand,* until no sooner than I finished the thought, she fell fast asleep. At first it was a gentle purr, but that became louder and louder until it was full blown snoring, stuttering, smacking lips—did she have a cleft pallet? Deviated septum? I know she probably could control little of her predicament, but I paid for my seat and this is nowhere in the fine print.

I made a rookie mistake: in my panic to shield my arms and secure the armrest, which continued to float up as gravity took hold and she settled, I didn't grab the headphones and now, pinned against the window, there was no way to bend forward and pull them out of my briefcase, sitting under the seat in front of me, where I had dutifully stowed them. In the best of circumstances, leaning forward without my head hitting the seat in front of me was difficult—on this day it would be impossible and the what if I got stuck down there with only her meaty calves to view? Nope, this was going to be unpleasant and I would just have to tough it out. At least we weren't delayed.

Then the captain came over the loudspeaker, saying we were delayed. Going to LaGuardia is always delayed. The upside is this gave me time to consider my options. There were no options. That's when, in her relaxed state of slumber, those giant arms propped up on her ample bosom started to slide. At first, her sloth-like reflexes caught them, and she'd jerk half awake and work them back up exposing her armpits, which, thankfully, had seen a razor—at least a few days ago. Ack! I threw up in my mouth a little bit.

But as time wore on, somewhere around 7:30 a.m., and the plane ambled to the tarmac, her depth of sleep overcame her reflexes and now the arms were free to plummet towards her adjacent passengers. They were literally hitting me in the chest. Tapping her on the shoulder to jar her out of her slumber was like a flea knocking on an elephant's hide—it was to no effect. This was going to call for a more aggressive approach.

I tried the elbow in the ribs—gently mind you, but at least it would get her to prop the arms back up on top. A little jab. It was like elbowing a giant, soft pillow. No resistance at all. My arm went so far in it was getting hot and I never made it to bone. I had to grab my own wrist to pull my arm back out. Okay, tactic two: keeping my arm bent in like a chicken wing, I gave a gentle uppercut to the bottom of her elbow, and that startled her enough to vacate the space that, after all, I paid for. The plane was now in a parked hold on the tarmac.

Well, as we waited and waited to take off, the sparring grew in intensity. The longer we sat, the quicker and deeper she seemed to drift back into relaxation, to the point where I was upper-cutting her elbow with mine hard enough to get air as her arms bounced and snort-cough her out of sleep; that actually drew sideways glares at me—like this was my fault! I could only keep this up so long, I was rusty and out of shape, I had to think of something new. I already asked the flight attendant if there were any other seats on the plane, which I was sympathetically informed there were not and, since the FAA didn't allow passengers to ride in the restroom, my options were limited.

I decided to risk a rule infraction and came up with the idea of reclining my seat while hers stayed in the upright position. This gained me a precious few inches of gap from the surface of her seat to the surface of mine to at least carve out a niche my shoulder could sort-of fit in. This was not so bad, at least her elbow was out in front a bit more now and my shoulder, half in her armpit, was warmed to keep it loose. I leaned back.

Now, being as tall as I am, my neck hits about three-quarters of the way up the headrest, and the back of my head was exposed to the seat behind. *Wisp.* What in the hell just whisked my hair? *Wisp.* A few minutes later, there it was again... was that a newspaper? The guy behind me was apparently reading a newspaper, fully opened and as he turned the pages, it whisked my hair. Really? I mean, really? In a crowed plane, what, you can't fold the paper down and read it in quarters?

After the third pass, I spun in my seat and looked back. I know he saw me, but no reaction. No apology. No acknowledgement. Well, he has to know what he's done. *Wisp.* No way this is innocent. Does he somehow know the behemoth next to me and is taking umbrage at my tactics? There's no way, although between her snorting, coughing, and hacking, and my grunting to put enough weight behind my elbow uppercuts, who knows?

Wisp. That's it. I turn in my seat, look back at this guy—a professorial type with a short-cropped beard, bowtie, John Lennon style glasses—probably a tweed jacket but, I can't confirm that now, because my focus was locked on the whites of his eyes. We stared at each other for a good ten to fifteen seconds. That doesn't sound like a long time but, stop what you are doing and stare at something while slowly counting to ten. It's a long stare. Not a word is spoken. Just blank faces staring into each other's eyes, my lips pursed, jaw muscles grinding, nostrils flaring slightly as I breathed in and out.

My stare-down is interrupted by a meaty elbow in my back. I slowly turned back around, this has to be the end of the newspaper assault. Other than I was calling him out on his poor newspaper reading etiquette, why else would we have stared each other down? *Wisp*. How many pages are in this newspaper?

Now it is on. A plan formulated in my mind. An uppercut once again reseats the fleshy flyer's arm back up on her massive heaving bosom, leaving my hand up, even with my neck, pinky finger resting against my cheek. My senses now tuned in to the crinkle of the newspaper, I waited. Then as the wisp started, I shot my hand back over my shoulder, behind my headrest and grabbed the paper. I yanked it forward into my seat and wadded it up in a ball. In one fluid motion, like I'm giving someone the "up yours" sign with my left hand in the crook of my elbow as my right shot the wadded-up newspaper past my right ear, I hurled it back to Mr. Bowtie.

I know from the trajectory it had struck home, but I neither turned to confirm it, nor do I say a word. Neither does he. I never saw his expression—whether it was one of surprise or incredulity, I do not know. I never heard a word. We never spoke. But his paper never whisked my hair again.

I sometimes wondered what he must have thought. I think he had to know what he was doing, but did he? Maybe he was just sitting there reading a paper, biding his time while we were delayed on the tarmac and then, out of the blue, some whack-job snatched his paper out of his hands, quickly wadded it up and shot it back into his chest.

Was he actually a professor who now had fodder for his next lesson on holding one's temper, or maybe a member of the clergy, who could use this to illustrate getting along with your neighbor in his next sermon? I would love to know how he told his story about the plane ride out of Atlanta and the passenger that grabbed his newspaper, wadded it up and threw it back at him.

As to the 380 lb. muumuu-wearing narcoleptic with razor stubble armpits, I don't know what became of her either. I climbed out over the seat in front of me when the plane eventually landed and, for all I know, she's still stuck between the armrests that held her fast—or maybe she's had to go through life with the seats still attached to her buxom booty; it wouldn't surprise me.

The whole thing was like a bad version of *The Twilight Zone's:* "Nightmare at 20,000 feet," where William Shatner flies for the first time since his nervous breakdown and swears he sees a gremlin on the wing of the plane, except it was more like twenty feet and my gremlin was like Jabba the Hutt inside the plane.

"You're traveling through another dimension—a dimension not only of sight and sound but of mind... your next stop; the Twilight Zone!"
[Rod Serling ~ The Twilight Zone ~ 1963]

—Chapter Sixteen—

Got my Cheez Whiz, Boy? — 2009

Elwood, Jake & the Bluesmobile ~ ©1980 The Blues Brothers

When the Blues Brothers hit theaters in 1980, I must have seen that movie ten times and a hundred since. Doesn't break my Star Wars record of twenty-one in the theater in 1977, but it is one my all-time favorite flicks. I had seen the Blues Brothers band on Saturday Night Live and loved their sound, but at fifteen years old, I wasn't even driving, legally, yet. I saw the movie, the first time, with a bunch of friends in our church youth group, when we were on an Appalachian service project in Tennessee. And I was totally hooked!

One of my buddies (I'll call him "Fitz" to protect the innocent) and I used lines from that movie hundreds of times, not the least of which was almost every time we were in a car together, one of us would start in our best Elwood impersonation, "It's a 106 miles to Chicago, we got a full tank of gas, half a pack of cigarettes, it's dark... and we're wearing sunglasses." And the other would finish with, "Hit it." I cannot tell you how many times we invoked, "We're on a mission from God." and flipped a Zippo lighter lid closed.

Some fifteen-odd years later, my dad and I were in Chicago, for a convention, on business and took some time to drive by his old stomping grounds on North Shore Drive. After I'd seen where he'd lived and was regaled with nostalgic memories like catching a play-ground swing in the forehead and almost bleeding out, we decided to take the famous route from the chase scene down under the el (elevated train) on Lower Whacker Drive. That was really cool, but amazingly shorter than it looks in the movie. To this day, the only address for a major league ballpark I think I've ever known is 1060 West Addison—the address for Wrigley Field, where the Cubs still play, and which Elwood had on his driver's license when he falsified his renewal. Classic.

Over the years, another buddy (I'll call him "Rog") joined in on the act, and often took the role of driver when Fitz and myself were, engaged elsewise. Like riding on the roof of the car to see if we could hold on at 100 mph; probably not our brightest moment. And whenever one of us was engaged with or spotted the local authori-ties, "Shit. What? Rollers. No. Yep. Shit." Or actually pulled over; "...I bet these cops got SCMODS. SCMODS? State – County – Municipal – Offender – Data – System." Every time!

As we grew older and more mature, we all married in the late 80s and 90s and focused on raising our own families, as folks do. But we always stayed loosely in touch, getting together a few times a year and eventually, that fell off to once a year or so. The drinking game of watching the movie and chugging a beer every time a police car wrecked, was in the distant past. But it's funny how when you are such good friends, years can go by and you pick up right where you left off—like no time had passed.

And that we would. Lines from old movies would come out in spades: from Stripes, Caddyshack, Animal House, but inevitably the one from The Blues Brothers where Elwood and Jake have just returned to Elwood's crappy apartment next to the el. Having been chased by the police and amidst all that is going on, this old guy playing cards sees Elwood out of the corner of his eye and says' "Ya got my Cheez Whiz, boy?" Elwood, without missing a beat fishes into his pocket and tosses over a can of Cheez Whiz. Subtle and absolutely hysterical.

"Ya got my Cheese-Whiz boy?" ~ ©*1980 The Blues Brothers*

We used that line ad nauseam all through the 1980s, usually after we'd bought a can of it and some crackers, and whenever one of us would need a hit, we'd deliver the line and whoever had the can would toss it across the room. Once we were all married and had growing kids of our own, the movie line references faded with more important things to catch up on. A bygone era gone by.

By the time 2000 rolled around, we'd gotten together less and less as we each were involved with families, kid's sports or other events. Sometimes, a few—or several years would go by before we'd hook back up. And in 2009 it had been a few years. Fitz was flying solo, his wife on parenting duty at one of his kid's events, and so was tasked with bringing an appetizer. I was already there when he walked in with his bag of whatever, and before I even asked how he and the family had been the last several years, I said, "Ya got my Cheez Whiz, boy?" Without missing a beat, twenty-nine years later, he reached into the bag, grabbed a can and tossed it across the room!

How classic was that? I'll bet it had been ten years since we'd last used that line, and bam! Picked right up like it was yesterday. I would be hard pressed to tell you what his kids or wife, or mine for that matter, were doing in 2009, but I remember that like it was yesterday!

"Here's to good friends, tonight is kinda of special."
[Arthur Prysock, American Jazz Singer ~ 1924–1997 ~
Löwenbräu commercial circa 1977]

—Chapter Seventeen—

You Betcha!—2010

Chisholm-Hibbing (HIB) Airport —ironically, with a white Ford parked out front

Hibbing was not a place I'd heard of before, when I had to make a business trip there, in early 2010. It is a city of about 17,000 in St. Louis County, Minnesota, just West of Lake Superior, built on the rich iron ore of the Mesabi Iron Range and boasts the largest open-pit iron mine in the world. It is also the home of Bob Dylan in the state of 10,000 lakes. Flying in, I believed there were that many lakes—they were everywhere, as far as the eye could see.

I connected from a flight out of Minneapolis-St. Paul airport. It's a nice airport, not too big and plenty of nice folks, but we had landed a little late and I was in a hurry to make the connection, so I didn't really pay too much attention to my surroundings. I found my gate with little effort and they were just calling "first class" when I walked up. I had been upgraded with my Medallion status, which happened about fifty-percent of the time I flew in those days. Usually, an upgrade to first means you're in a larger seat where cocktails are served, and you might get a meal, depending on the length of the flight and the time of day. I gave my ticket to the gate agent and ambled down the jet-way.

The jet-way ended, not stepping onto the plane as I was accustomed to, but at a stairway that led to the tarmac and that to another stairway, which was in fact, the door of the plane opened downward. Okay, it had been a few years—maybe twenty-some odd years, since I was in a plane this small, but no biggie. As I climbed up into the plane (not sure how a handicapped person would have gotten up the stairs), I had to bend at a thirty degree angle to walk through the cabin—I'm a tall guy, not overly tall, but used to having to duck and tilt my head in planes, in this one I had to bend at the waist.

I found my seat in first class, which on this plane meant, you got to sit down first. Class is relative on a small plane, and on this flight, there was no distinction between classes—sort of like lyrics from a Bob Dylan song: *we are all the same*. They called the next boarding zone and the other seven passengers filed aboard. The captain climbed aboard next and as I glanced up, he looked distantly familiar. Oh yeah, he was the gate agent who just took my ticket. A bit unusual, but certainly efficient and no union prima donnas here.

Once the cabin door was pulled up by the flight attendant and secured, the captain made an announcement — by turning his head over his shoulder and bellowing. Apparently, we had a slight weight displacement that needed to be corrected. I'm thinking they'll move luggage around in the hold, or maybe there were ballast tanks like on a boat that they would use to adjust the balance. Nope. Passenger, 1A, please move to seat 2B. We need a volunteer who's in front of row 3 to move behind row 5 and then once airborne you can move back to your seat...WTF? (Wry Tonnage Figuring)

Once the balance was set, and it seemed we were ready for push-back, a rumbling started in my seat. It was a sustained vibration and I thought, well, you must get a magic fingers massage here in "first class." I put my Kindle down and gazed out the window at a prop that was spinning up to speed. This was a bit of a surprise since I have been on jets for the last couple of decades and had not flown on a prop plane since the late 1980s.

I looked across to watch the other engine fire up. The other engine didn't fire up. We taxied out with only one engine running. Which was alarming at best, but they had to know this, and I didn't want to seem the novice, so I casually rested one arm on the armrest and with the other reached back to tuck my shirt into my underwear to absorb the sweat running down my back. But once we hit the runway, the other engine sputtered then roared to life and off we went. Pretty cool, really.

The flight was not cool. I am one of those roller coaster guys who have no problem with drops that put the pit of your stomach in your throat, or a wind-shear here or there — I am not a white-knuckle flyer at all. Usually the sound of the engines puts me right to sleep and I only awake if that piercing "ding!" denoting cruising altitude goes off right above my head. I was actually enjoying the scenery until we started the approach to Chisholm Airport near Hibbing, then those rollercoaster rides came back to the forefront with abandon—actually, it was more like the Great Gasp at Six Flags on a broken shoot that kept yanking up and down.

For those of you unfamiliar with that particular attraction, The Great Gasp was a 225-foot-tall Intamin Paratower, a "Parachute Drop" ride, that towered over Six Flags Over Georgia for almost thirty years. It became a beacon for the park during this time. The ride was dismantled and removed from the park in 2005, sometime after it broke while I happened to be riding it. In the vernacular of northern Minnesota: yee-hah and you betcha!

We did at least land on a paved runway—there are options for grass at Chisholm—and taxied on in to the terminal. I quickly made my way through the terminal, past the other gate, past baggage claim, and to ground transportation. It was quick because it was all in the same room. I went out to find my rental car, only to find no rental cars. The company travel agent had alerted me to the fact that, in some of these smaller airports, this was a possibility, and so I was prepared with the rental car company's number in hand.

I called Travis' Rent-a-Car with my reservation number handy and on the other end of the line was—Travis. I asked if he could transfer me to customer service, and he said, "Oh, hi there. No need for a transfer, is this John? We were expecting your call, then." I told him I was at the airport and needed the car, to which he replied, "Oh, you betcha. We'll get a vehicle right over to ya, on the double. Have it to ya in a jip!"

I started to take a stroll around the outside of the terminal. Why do they call it *terminal*? As if fear of flying isn't bad enough on its own. Within two minutes, a white Ford came barreling up the driveway and this young guy hops out, "You must be John, there, yeah?" I said I was, and he introduced himself as Travis. Nice enough guy, very outgoing and accommodating. Seeing not a lot of other cars around and no one else in sight, I asked if he needed a ride back to the rental office? "Oh no," he says with pride, "we got multiple cars here; we got a whole fleet of six!" A whole fleet of six.

I guess everything's relative. I thanked him and started off on my day. In hindsight, it was such a warm and genuine experience, I wish I had found time to enjoy the folks and local culture a bit more — it's impossible not to fall in love with those Minnesota accents. You betcha!

"All you need in this life is ignorance and confidence, and then success is sure."
[Mark Twain ~ 1835–1910 ~ American Author]

—Chapter Eighteen—

You Betcha! The Return Trip Then—2010

Bustling HIB

From the previous chapter, "You Betcha!" This, as the late great Paul Harvey used to say, is the rest of the story.

After my flight and rental car experience coming into Hibbing,

Minnesota, I eventually had to make my way back home. I was looking forward to interacting with some of the locals, even if for just a short time waiting in the airport. Unfortunately, I hadn't had enough time to explore anything, not even visit Bob Dylan's home. No sightseeing at all. Couldn't even find a song of his on the radio. Which just confirms: *"It slips away, and all your money won't another minute buy. Dust in the wind. All we are is duuuuust in the wiiiiind."*

I have to say; getting through Atlanta-Hartsfield (ATL), which is the busiest airport in the world at over one-hundred-million passengers per year and a sprawl of 4,700 acres and Minneapolis—St. Paul at over thirty-seven million passengers, navigating Chisholm-Hibbing was like taking candy from a baby. They average about 9,000 passengers a year—that's 24 per day.

But I didn't think about that in allowing timing for departing. At ATL, with Clear Pass or TSA Pre-Check, you can usually get through check-in and security comfortably inside an hour. I typically allow one-and-a-half to two hours to be safe—a little more if it's a heavy travel day. My subconscious mental calculations allowing time in an unfamiliar airport to drop the car, get through security, maybe grab a cold one and catch a part of some game on TV, give it a good hour, maybe one-and-a-half. At HIB, I needed two. Minutes.

Yep, my pal Travis from the rental car place said, "Sure, just leave the car right out front, there. Should be just fine, you betcha." What about the keys? Leave them on the tire? "Ha! That's a good one John. No, just leave 'em under the floormat and lock the car door then. We've got another set and will open 'er right up when we get there!" Okay, you betcha.

I left the car out front and walked into the airport to find the check-in line. There was no check-in line. There was no agent to check you in. There was no one around to ask who checks you in. There was, literally no one. Not another soul in the entire airport. What in tarnation? I looked at my watch, right time zone. I walked in through an open front door, but every kiosk—two of them, and every counter was locked up. Did the airport close since this morning? Were there only flights in the a.m. and I misunderstood the "p.m." on my itinerary? It was like I was in one of those movies where you're the last man on earth. Like Charlton Heston in The Omega Man. And the 1971 movie, not the 2007 remake I Am Legend with Will Smith. Well, whatever your era, you get the idea.

I mean, I was just in this airport not seven hours ago. And it was bustling. Travis the rental guy brought my car right to me and knew me by name, never mind I was the only person standing in front of the terminal. Okay, bustling may be a slight exaggeration, but there were people. No worries, right? I'll just find the bar and have a beer and wait to check-in. I turned 120° to my right and found the bar / snack shop / restaurant …closed. Quiet. Eerily devoid of anything living.

It would have only been creepier if there was no cell signal. But there was. So, I wandered around the terminal, took a few phone shots—this was pre-selfie days, or I would have gotten a sweet shot with the seven-foot tall grizzly in the waiting area. Sent them off to my boss who just told me to hang in there. I called out once or twice but only received my echo. I was about to cue up a Bob Dylan song when another human finally entered the airport.

He wasn't as talkative as Travis. He actually just gave me one of those nods that just says, "Hey, but keep your distance—I don't know you." But then a ticket agent showed up and fired up her computer and I ran over to be first in line, in front of the other guy, and got checked in. She was really nice, had that same great accent and seemed pretty darn efficient there. I just watched her for a while which probably creeped her out. Mr. nod just gave a quick head-bob and went back to reading his phone. After about forty-five minutes there were a few more travelers, but not a lot of official-looking personnel.

By now, enough time had gone by that we were not too far away from boarding time, and I'm thinking *it's odd we haven't gone through the security area that has still got a lock on the metal detector*. There's no one to be seen for this part of the process, but pretty soon the ticket agent walked over, so I asked if someone will be here from the TSA since it looks shutdown. She says, "Yep, have that for ya in jiff." Okay then. Then she literally takes off her ticket agent hat and puts on a TSA hat and badge and proceeded to unlock the metal detector. I had to chuckle. Out loud.

She looked over and gave me a wink, then goes into the standard boarding spiel you hear every time you go through security about liquids in separate bags, pull your laptop out of your bag, etc. Except this time, it was totally enjoyable because I felt like I was on the set of Fargo. "So, that was Mrs. Lundegaard on the floor in there. And I guess that was your accomplice in the wood chipper?" Then we're through to the one gate at the airport and I'm thinking if she's the ticket agent and the TSA Agent, is she the gate agent too? You betcha!

She literally switched hats back to the airline hat and started the boarding process. Hysterical and impressive, all at the same time. She got everyone through the gate — by everyone, I mean the five of us. We headed out towards the plane. The turboprop. The line sort of stalled at the end of the jet way, which is the end of painted lines on the tarmac, and then she scooted in front and she and the captain escorted us up the stairs into the cabin. I mentioned that she should be getting paid for working three jobs and she just smiled at me. I found my seat, looked up and see she's also the flight attendant closing the boarding door; make that four jobs. Got to just love it!

"Always remember that you are absolutely unique. Just like everyone else."
[Margaret Mead ~ 1901–1978 ~ American Scientist]

—Chapter Nineteen—

Donny and Maureen—2010

Our 2010 Christmas Card: The Donny & Maureen Show

New York is an incredible city. I am certainly no world traveler, but I've seen my fair share of big cities and smaller ones too. New York is unique in so many ways. From the lights and bawdiness of Times Square, to the staggering number of people who are always moving about—over eight million; what could all these people possibly do for a living?

From the majesty of the Statue of Liberty and the grandeur of the Empire State Building, to Central Park. Add to that the Hollywood fanfare, and filming, and recording of shows, and the Theatre District—amazing. It's a lot compacted onto one fairly small island, but I guess that's what makes it so unique.

I took my wife, Maureen, there for her first time on vacation with some good friends of ours in late December 2010, and we stayed at the Marriott Marquis in crazy Times Square. Also performing at the Marriott, in a Christmas musical, was Donny Osmond.

Donny is about five years older than Maureen and me, and we grew up watching the the *Donnie & Marie Show* along with *The Jackson 5* in the mid-1970s on TVs that had rabbit ear antennas and all of six or seven channels—the dark ages to most Millennials. Maureen still has quite a few Donny Osmond record albums in a box somewhere in the basement.

For those born in the digital era, that is how we used to listen to music: off of a vinyl disk called a record, that had the musical tracks literally carved into it. They were played on a device called a record player that had a turntable, which had an arm with a needle on the end of it that you set in the groove on the record and selected the speed to play the recording back. There was no Spotify or Pandora to setup playlists or search for music by genre, and no FF or skipping a tune you didn't like. You just planted yourself in one spot and played the songs in order.

You didn't take your music with you in those days and could never have carried the record player and listened with headphones (earbuds didn't exist yet) even if you wanted to. Had you tried, the needle would have scratched the record with the turntable up on your shoulder and extension cords would only get you so far anyway, since the mobile battery hadn't been invented either. To appreciate the older records from the 40s, 50s and 60s, you had to tune your ear to filter out the hissing and scratching.

Holy crap are we old; it's like we hadn't even landed on the moon yet! Let's not get carried away; we had landed on the moon at least five years earlier. So, we just sat in our beanbag chairs and chilled out to "Go Away Little Girl."

Yep, those were the days.

Donny's musical run flattened out in the 80s, but he has always been talented and, he and his sister have been performing for the better part of fifty years. She even danced on *Dancing with the Stars* (a reality ballroom dancing show where the celebrities dance with professionals) and two seasons later, Donny followed suit, winning the title and coveted Mirror Ball trophy.

So anyway, our friends (I'm going to change their names to protect their identities and embarrassment by association [to Maureen of course]; we'll call them: "Ralph" and "Nancy") Ralph and Nancy arrived ahead of us that first night in the lobby. As Maureen is too shy, Nancy is too bold. Nancy has no problem approaching strangers to chat, ask a question, or just converse—especially if they are famous in any way. Nancy is no novice in rubbing elbows with the stars. She had already struck up a conversation with Donny and had Ralph take her picture with him, before we made it to the lobby.

When we arrived and heard this, Maureen told Nancy what a huge fan of Donny's she was and how she loved his albums and loved his songs. She got giddy just talking about him. It figured with our luck, she didn't get to see Nancy get her picture taken with him.

But, as we lamented the near miss of seeing Maureen's teen idol, and starting to relive the 70s, who should be walking across the other side of the lobby, but Donny.

Maureen was flushed just getting a glimpse from across the room and all atwitter that she got to see not only someone famous, but her childhood crush! Nancy would have none of that, "from across the lobby" stuff. When Maureen wouldn't go over to him, Nancy sauntered over to Donny, and grabbed him by the elbow.

He had to interrupt his cell phone call as she pulled him over, explaining that one of his biggest fans was right over there, and he could call back whoever he was talking to. So as Maureen stood rooted right where she was, both enthralled and aghast, Nancy dragged Donny across the lobby to us and introduced Maureen as a huge fan that he had to take a picture with.

He was generously saying, "Sure, I'd love to," when Maureen gushed, "I just love you!" I am sure he's heard this a thousand times, and put his arm around Maureen, who had turned three shades of pink-to-red and was grinning like the Cheshire Cat. I was amused she just said that to him, as I had been around stars many times in the past and knew how to handle these situations.

As I coolly got my camera ready to take the shot, I couldn't help myself, and, unable to think of anything poignant to say, blurted out, "You totally deserved to win Dancing with the Stars; you were awesome!" Oh boy. Donny's smile seemed a little more forced, and Ralph looked sideways at me in disgust and asked, "What are you, president of his fan club?" and then added "...dork."

With my steely resolve in tatters, shredded by star-struck embarrassment, all I could do was snap the shot. It was a great picture, capturing the down-to-earth Donny, who posed politely with his arm around his biggest fan, and Maureen looked like the teenage crush had never left. Donny shied away, continuing with his call, as we laughed about our great moment and how cool we both were; especially me.

We used the shot that next year as our annual Christmas card; the rest of the family positioned in the background looking askance at a star-struck Maureen and her childhood crush. Come to think of it, Maureen doesn't look this happy in our wedding pictures.

But then, I'm a little bit country and she's a little bit rock 'n roll.

"I don't deserve any credit for turning the other cheek as my tongue is always in it."
[Flannery O'Connor ~ 1925–1964 ~ American Author]

—Chapter Twenty—

Silverleaf
Shenanigans—2011

Silverleaf Clubhouse from the 18th Tee ~ circa 2011

There are untold stories, never put to pen and paper, only passed down through the spoken word. These tales are expounded upon and embellished, never documented, and, over time, impossible to confirm, thus becoming lore. This is one of those stories that in all likelihood should remain uttered only in hushed tones, preferably over a cocktail.

In February of 2004, we began an annual, friendly, golf tournament hosted and put together by a good friend, Ralph Scatena. The tournament was played at beautiful courses out West, in and around Scottsdale, Arizona. It was so named *The Scatena Desert Invitational, Tournament of AZ holes*. It has since become legend and everyone who hears of it asks to be on the short list, should any participant dropout. That has only happened twice, once, at the loss of a job in the early years, before it was clear what an incredible junket it was to become, and once, by literally passing away. No doubt about it; it is not easy to get in.

We have played spectacular courses, set in incredible landscapes, that are both daunting and stunning at the same time. And out of nearly every Invitational comes a classic tale, one of my favorites unfolded in 2011.

We were invited to play at one of the most exclusive golf clubs in the heart of North Scottsdale: Silverleaf Club. Tucked into the canyons of the McDowell Mountains and surrounded by the McDowell Sonoran Preserve, the private club features a Tom Weiskopf designed, eighteen-hole championship golf course that winds along 7,322 yards of inspiring terrain. The 50,000 square-foot Rural Mediterranean-style Silverleaf Clubhouse is highlighted by world class spa facilities, resort and lap pools, fully appointed men's and women's locker rooms, as well as fine and casual dining.

Upon arrival, in the auto courtyard, guests are greeted by a beautiful fountain that was originally discovered in the southwestern corner of France bordering Spain. The fountain, which was most likely once used as a functional source of drinking water for villagers, now welcomes members and guests with unique sophistication.

So, as we arrived in our Kia rental car, with four large guys sand-wiched in to make room for our oversized golf bags, being our first time to the club, we unknowingly turned just short of the auto courtyard. Had we known at the time about the fountain, we would have looked for that as a telltale landmark in our approach.

We drove up the pristine cobblestone driveway, into a covered garage and as our eyes adjusted to the light, we noticed several valets with their hands up shouting at us to stop. Thinking this a bit odd, we started to get out of the car. As it turns out, we were in the golf cart barn. They were not valets, they were the cart barn staff. This place was not only above our paygrade, but our status and station in life in general. Essentially, we mistook the Caddy Shack for the Clubhouse.

Recovering from our astonishment at the grandest of golf cart barns I've ever laid eyes on, I felt like we should tip these guys just for driving into it. We gave them each two dollars and cautiously backed out, driving on to the auto courtyard where four attendants appeared from nowhere and opened our four doors simultaneously.

Not wanting to appear as commoners, we casually tossed the keys to one of them and asked them not to scratch it. They smiled politely, adding no retort. They waved us off from carrying our own clubs from the back of the car, shock on their faces apparent. Not sure if this was purely etiquette or more likely so we didn't bang the Maserati, Rolls Royce, Lamborghini, or Ferrari neatly parked in a semicircle around the French fountain.

Our usual modus operandi is to save time by pulling our shoes or flip-flops off as we exit the vehicle, grabbing our golf shoes from the back of the car and putting them on with one foot up on the bumper. When it became apparent that we might actually do this, the *Master* Valet discretely informed us there were guest lockers in the men's locker quarters if we could kindly replace our footwear there. Stifling a comment about this seeming inefficient, we complied.

Apparently, these highfalutin clubs also have a dress code. Proper attire includes slacks, golfing shorts, no shorter than four inches above the knee, golf shirts with collars *and* sleeves, sweaters and jackets. Not permitted are cutoffs, jeans, running shorts, cargo pants or cargo shorts, T-shirts, undershirts, sweat suits, jogging suits, and tennis attire. We were the posterchildren for attire not permitted.

Cargo shorts became a sticking point. One of our golfers, (we'll call him Dan to protect his identity), at the time was sporting cargo shorts. Years later, he would become one of our best dressed. But on this day, his particular canvas cargo shorts had big pockets. Big baggy pockets—but at least they were not camo. He liked to have ample storage for various golfing accoutrements and a place to collect golf balls when he found them. His pockets could collectively store thirty-two golf balls. At least he donned a collared shirt after being shamed out of his T-shirt back at the Resort.

The general manager discretely pulled our host, Ralph, aside. In a voice with mob-like undertones, he informed Ralph the "gentleman" in cargo shorts was not permitted to play, dressed as such. Either Ralph could tell him, or he would. Ralph elected to run interference.

Dan was a down-to-earth sort of guy. No highbrow Country Club snob was going to tell him how to dress. But the round was being comp'd for the eight of us at about $350 a pop; so, we eased into a quiet corner of the expansive courtyard, so as to not make a scene. We talked Dan into buying a pair of proper length golfing shorts in the pro shop. Make sure they were within four inches of the knee we quipped. This garnered not even a smile from Dan.

Dan shortly emerged from the pro shop still in his cargo shorts; no way in hell was he paying ninety-five dollars for a pair of shorts he could buy at Wal-Mart for fourteen-ninety-nine. We were running out of options and our tee time was nearing. No one had brought extra shorts, but rain pants were allowed. One of us loaned him a pair of polyester, non-breathing Gore-Tex rain pants. He decided to wear those over his cargo shorts until he was out of site of the pro shop and then would just take them off.

We had caddies. Who were also members of the club and pretty much scratch golfers. Dan's plan was not going to fly. So, even though it was 102° in the desert, Dan saved the ninety-five dollars and played all eighteen holes in the rain paints. He lost 14 lbs. that day. He squished at the end of the round from the sweat soaking his shoes.

We gave the caddies a workout too. One of them finally said, as he labored in his fifteenth or sixteenth sand trap, "Sir. Can you *please* walk out on the same path you walked in?" It was not a question. In our defense, it's tough when your shot dribbles into a trap, then you hit it two feet further into the trap. Bury it under the lip on the third shot, and eventually have to punchout sideways. But it is a lot of raking.

We were allowed to play one more time the following year, but then, Ralph was asked not to bring the "guests from Georgia," back to the club. This was both amusing and sad, because it is a spectacular venue and one you can only be invited to.

The following picture is from the eighteenth hole of that final outing.

Silverleaf 18 Green — circa 2012

"There is an old saying: if a man comes home with sand in his cuffs and cockleburs in his pants, don't ask him what he shot."
[Sam Snead ~ 1912–2002 ~ American Professional Golfer]

—Chapter Twenty-One—

The Bow—2012

*Our 2012 Christmas Card featuring Madniss practicing
with "The Bow"*

There are times in life when, no matter how hard you try, destiny
cannot be altered. You may be able to affect the outcome of
certain immediate aspects of life, but, like throwing a rock into a
river, the ripple and splash do not change the flow of water or alter
its course. What is meant to be, will be.

Back when our daughter, Madison, was sweet sixteen, after beseeching us for years, she convinced her mother and I to let her delve into the world of archery. She had stayed with this pursuit longer than any previously, and she finally got her mother to yield. Even under intense batting of teenage eyelashes, I still wasn't persuaded, until I went to a higher authority; I read The Hunger Games.

For those of you who have not read, seen, or heard of The Hunger Games, one, you may want to broaden your horizons, and two, very few quickly develop the cunning and accuracy as does the main character, Katniss Everdeen. Katniss is a great heroine and inspired many a young lady to get involved in the world of archery. I once asked Madison if that was what got her into wanting to shoot arrows, but she said no, she had watched my dad shoot for years and was enamored more from that.

Since I had a bow and arrows myself and knew how exciting and dangerous it could be, I was willing to invest in this archery gambit. And when I agree to fund such forays, I reserve the right to bestow nicknames; Madison now has to suffer being called *Madniss*. She shoulders it well.

Madniss signed up for lessons and joined a club and took up Olympic Recurve style archery. There are all kinds and levels of archery: there is bare-bow, which means no sights, triggers, or stabilizers—only the bow, arrows, and your fingers.

There is compound archery, which outfits a bow with cam-wheels that reduce draw tension, multiple sights and scopes, triggers that are used to release—typically used for hunting. Being Recurve archers, we call compounds "bows with training wheels," or "cheater-bows." But what Madniss chose is what you see in the Olympics: a recurve bow with one sight and stabilizer, no triggers or cams

As she got into archery, it turned out Madniss had a natural affinity for it. She shot untrained for several months and then a level five (highest) coach spotted her. Turns out she had the right physical makeup as Olympians do: long neck, correctly proportioned arm length for full draw, etc. So as her coach began to help her with form, we looked into taking this to a competitive level.

Once you're out of the base level equipment, it turns out you can drop some serious cash getting outfitted to compete nationally. We were not flush with cash. Times were tough in 2012 and we were amassing debt just making it by month-to-month. We were told, and it's true, that if you're going to commit to this level of archery, sooner or later you're going to upgrade the riser (the center part of the bow), the limbs, kind of bowstring, arrows, vanes, or spin-wings, and on and on and on.

The best way to get outfitted correctly, if you can afford it, is to bite it off all at once, so you train on the best equipment you're eventually going to compete with. This keeps you from having to readjust and learn each time something changes. The minutest change over sixty meters can mean missing the target entirely.

Believe me, I know, because I eventually took up archery too and little Madniss is a way more skilled archer than her dear ol' dad. Well, sadly for our little Madniss, buying the right bow wasn't going to happen. Christmas was fast approaching and paying the bills took precedence.

This is where that twist of fate makes clear the path of destiny.

I was a client to a vendor I was working with up in Michigan, just north of Detroit. I was overseeing a fairly large project that had me at their facility for several days. So, one evening, we decided to hit the MGM Grand Casino for dinner and a little gambling. Now, I'm a pretty good eater and I've been known to enjoy a cocktail or two, but I am not a gambler.

Don't get me wrong, I love gambling, I bet on my own mother's tennis matches when I was thirteen. Love to play poker with the boys. Love playing the betting pools during football season. But in a casino—I'm no good. I've been up numerous times in casinos, but at the end of the day, they always want me to come back and give them more of my money. I am a sucker for Blackjack, but rarely have I left a casino in the positive.

The owner of the company I was working with was a big gambler. A real high-dollar player; everybody in the casino knew his name. He'd won tens of thousands and lost them too. My colleague, John, and I watched him play at a high-stakes Blackjack table for a while and he was on a hot streak. He must have had eight or ten grand stacked up in front him. He asked us to sit, and I had to confess I'd never even seen a $500 table, much less sat at one. Five-dollar tables were way more my speed. After politely declining the third or fourth time and telling him I just didn't have money to lose, he handed me and John each $300 in chips and said to go find a table, chips were on him. Win it, lose it, it was ours—but go have fun.

Oh... play with someone else's money? Didn't have to tell me twice. John and I found a more reasonable table to play at—a twenty-five dollar table. We began playing and I was winning a few hands, losing a few more; about the same as always. I had been telling John about our plight, trying to scrape together enough money to buy Maddie a real bow so she could compete at the highest level one day and what all was involved. He looked over at me after about an hour, when I was up, and said, "You should play for the bow."

Not a bad idea. A moral reason to gamble. "Whatever you win when playing for the bow, pull it aside and don't bet with that money any more—what you win goes towards the bow," he opined. In my best Elwood Blues, Chicago-clipped accent I retorted, "We're on a mission from God."

This particular table had the usual two-to-one insurance and Blackjack paid three-to-two, but it also had some long-odd sucker side-bets. Never tell me the odds! So almost every time I played for the bow, I won and often hit Blackjack. Whenever I did, I pulled that money aside and it became a thing—I'd take winnings from "my" hand and play for the bow, and bam! Blackjack. I didn't want to jinx anything, so I didn't play for the bow every time, just when it felt right. And we were having fun, so it needed to last a little while.

But after some time went by and playing for the bow was obviously a winning strategy, John goes, "Why not play the ten-to-one side bet for the bow on this one?" The ten-to-one bet was a minimum of twenty-five dollars and it was a one-time bet; either you hit Blackjack and won on the deal or you lost it—it didn't ride. I said, "Okay, for sweet little Madniss and the bow. Besides, we're on a mission from God." Blackjack! $250 in the bow fund.

We were hooting and hollering and began to draw a crowd. Whenever I felt the bow calling, I played for it and then the onlookers would cheer along with us. Twice I put fifty dollars on the sucker bet for the bow and won. Probably five times, I put money on it for me, to justify winning more for the bow of course and never won... fate?

Eventually I ran out of my own money and unwilling to reinvest the winnings from the bow fund, we called it a night. What a great night for my little archer, although she wouldn't know it yet. When I got back home from the trip, I told my wife about the winnings and we debated paying down the amassing pile of bills. But I specifically won that money playing for the bow. Tempting though it was to pay off some debt, we decided it was destiny that it should go towards the bow.

I called Madniss in and told her the story of gambling in a casino for the bow. In dramatic fashion on my high horse, I declared how this was not a lesson on how to win ill-gotten gains, as fortuitous as it turned out to be, but about using evil winnings for good. In all seriousness, I told her that if she was truly committed to archery and was not going to move on to something else in two months, I had won enough to buy the bow. She promised she would stick to it. She looked apprehensively at me as I pulled out a wad of one hundred-dollar bills and counted off twenty-eight of them. Combined with what she'd saved, Madniss purchased her Olympic level Hoyt recurve and took her first steps into a larger world.

'Gambling: The sure way of getting nothing for something.'
[Wilson Mizner ~ 1876–1933 ~ American Dramatist]

—Chapter Twenty-two—

The Great
Raccoon War—2014

Kevin the Raccoon in action ~ circa 2014

E veryone has, or knows someone, who has battled a pesky
wild animal. Some took it to another level with bigger pesky
wild animals and made TV shows out of these experiences like
Marlin Perkins's Mutual of Omaha's Wild Kingdom (that I watched
religiously through the 1970s and '80s) or more recently, Steve
Erwin's The Crocodile Hunter.

Some never went the fame and fortune route and just secured a place in family lore. For my father-in-law, it was those damn squirrels on his bird feeders. There is a whole 'nother story coming about the Great Squirrel Wars of the 80s; it was the best of times, it was the worst of times, it was the age of wisdom, it was the age of foolishness.

My particular nemesis was a stinking raccoon (Procyon lotor). Rotten little bugger was after my woman's birdseed. They may seem cute with their little whiskers and bandit mask and banded tails (made famous as a coonskin hat by Davy Crockett after he killed him a few). Even though they are supposedly smaller cousins to the bear family, I say they are more likened to oversized rats. They lurk stealthily in the dark; little nocturnal miscreants.

I never gave him a name—and Ricky is too obvious. For the purposes of this communiqué, let's go with Kevin. Kevin was crafty. He showed up—seemingly out of nowhere, usually around sundown when the haze of sunset would distort your vision. We had a dog to fend off such rodents: my trusty coon-dog, Riley. You would have hoped she'd be a little more aggressive defending our home, but she was getting up there in years in 2014 and defense of birdfeeders was apparently fairly low on the "that's my job" list.

We had several birdfeeders along our back-deck railing. Different shapes and sizes including a hummingbird feeder and a little birdbath that my father-in-law, Veteran of the Great Squirrel War, had made. It was a place where birds could break from their busy tasks of hunting for the family. A little bird sanctuary if you will—a space supposed to be safe from the likes of Kevin the raccoon. Our deck was off the back of our house standing about nine feet off the ground and had a straight set of stairs up the back, paralleling a screened-in porch that opened to it. That was the only way onto it, unless you were coming out of the house.

We usually knew when Kevin was stealing food because he would bang a birdfeeder against the railing as he jumped or stretched out to it. This noise would startle Riley, waking her from her nap and cause her to bark through the window with reckless abandon. I kept a .45-looking pellet pistol loaded and ready at the back door.

Kevin was destroying our bird sanctuary and needed to be taken out, but the problem was two-fold. One, there was a door from the family room to the screened-in porch, but to get a clean shot you had to open a second door from the porch to the deck. Two, Riley's barking and jumping at the full-length windows would alert Kevin to the imminent danger about to be inflicted on him and opening the first door let Kevin know it was not just Riley, held at bay by the window, but the expert marksman bearing down.

On occasion, when I'd try to sneak out the door, Riley would bully past, legs flailing as she tried to get her footing, which would make the shot even more difficult and usually Kevin would scamper to the deck railing and descend down the corner 6x6 post supporting the deck. Or would, on occasion, risk scooting by the porch door and down the set of stairs.

This was clever, because it caused me to navigate two doors and spin and shoot down the stairs at him. With wind variance, shadows and the elevation change, I usually overshot my target and reloading a pellet then giving it ten pumps gave the little bugger plenty of time to escape, off chuckling in the woods behind the house. I envision his laugh was probably snicker-y and sinister like Dick Dastardly's sidekick dog, Muttley.

127

After spotty on-and-off attacks over weeks, which drew into months, I concluded a new tactic was needed. Kevin was accustomed to Riley barking through the window, and as soon as the door was opened, would steal away into the night, sometimes without a shot even being fired. If the door wasn't opened, he would just look back over his shoulder at Riley and snicker.

My daughter, Madison, was amused by all of this and snapped the picture (above) of Kevin drinking from the birdbath as though he had casually bellied up to a bar, which only added insult to injury for me and Riley. Sometimes, Kevin would curl up in the birdbath if it was dry and bask in the afternoon sun.

This had to stop! Maureen loved her birds and hated that Kevin was so destructive, but she wasn't willing to sanction the hit. Like an armistice could be worked out between her, the birds, Kevin, Riley, and me. It was just too many factions with different motivations and desired outcomes.

Riley and I decided to go off the reservation and take matters into our own hands/paws. The new tactic would be a two-pronged attack. We would use a feign from Riley barking at the window (this came naturally to her) and I would sneak out the garage and come around from the corner of the house to draw a bead on the unsuspecting Kevin, with direct line of site to the feeders on the back railing.

While Riley and I strategized and worked out contingencies for our plan, the womenfolk just rolled their eyes. Riley never tried to talk me out of it, which I took as an affirmative she was on-board. Of course, Riley, being a dog, didn't talk, but let's not let details derail a good story.

On cue, about 8:30 p.m. or so Kevin showed up. One minute there were no hostiles, then the next, there he was. Climbing out onto the birdfeeder, his weight bending the arm the feeder hung from, twirling slowly around with total indifference to Riley, who, in full disclosure, had given up on her part of the plan and was just lying there at the window, scratching her back with all four in the air. Not a very ladylike pose either, mind you.

This was on me alone now; going rogue, I snuck quietly out the front door so as to not have the garage door make any sound and, went around the house. Faint light from the kitchen window splayed across Kevin, illuminating him perfectly. At the corner of the house was a small cedar tree for me to hide behind, but for the angle needed to take out Kevin, I also had to stretch out a little off-balance to get a clean shot. Lock and load.

As I leaned into the shot, I forgot about a motion sensor at the corner of the house and it inadvertently activated just as I cleared the tree. Two 150-watt halogen flood lights came fully to life illuminating not only me, but what turned out to be a giant three foot in diameter spider web with a really cool black and yellow four-inch-long spider dead center of the web about twenty inches from my face! I am telling you, no lie, that spider was big! (Following is a picture I took the next morning of that massive arachnid terror as proof.)

Arachnid Hell ~ the 2014 Great Raccoon War

I screamed like a schoolgirl and lost my footing. The barrel of the gun had punched through the spider web and set the whole thing rocking, the spider bouncing menacingly in the middle of it. At the same time, Kevin stopped eating birdseed, and looked casually up to see what the commotion was about and looked squarely at me. I doubt Riley was done scratching her back yet. Dammit! I refocused like a laser, after backing up a good foot because the spider scared the crap out of me and took the shot.

The pellet landed just below Kevin, embedded into one of the wooden railing balusters. I quickly reloaded and started pumping. By the time I brought the site to bear, Kevin was lumbering away down the stairs. But I gained some key intel. Kevin was making it up and down the stairs unnoticed because he blended perfectly into the shadow cast by the railing. That was how he seemed to appear out of thin air. That cunning little S.O.B. Now he was in for it!

So that night, about eleven o'clock, I poured a scotch and staked out a position on the back porch. I knew Kevin's meal had been interrupted and he'd be back. I was beginning to think like a raccoon. Maureen and Madison had given up on me; concluded I was nuts. Riley abandoned her post. It was just me and Kevin. I set the door ajar so I would have a clean sightline for the shot with my pellet pistol pumped and primed, lying across my lap.

I may have dozed off, but sometime close to midnight I heard the pitter-patter of little raccoon feet coming up the stairs right next to me. Kevin was staying in the shadows on his cautious climb, but I don't think he sensed I was there. Riley was asleep inside the door—she'd be useless in this battle and I had no way to alert her, and, even if I could, all she'd do is get Kevin snickering like Muttley again.

Our flank was exposed, but there was no aborting the mission now; all I needed was for that little bugger to head straight for the bird-feeders. Once he was up the stairs and cleared the doorframe, he'd be a sitting duck (mixing metaphors, I know). I had no compunction about shooting him in the back.

Kevin did the unthinkable. He didn't go for the birdseed straight ahead. He took a hard left and walked right into the screened in porch—apparently headed for Riley's dog food bowl and fresh water. WTF! He was less than three feet from the base of my chair!

I hadn't wanted to move before, thinking I might startle him and alert him to my presence, but now; we were both startled and looking eye to eye. I pointed the gun ready to put a third hole in that little raccoon mask and pulled the trigger. Nothing. The safety was on! He turned back around to make a swift exit. Crap! Now the game was afoot.

I flicked the safety off and fired, but in my panic over his proximity (way inside my personal space) and the safety miscue, I shot right underneath his little furry belly into the floor, almost shooting my own foot. By the time I could do anything else, Kevin was sauntering down the stairs, and all I could hear as he retreated into the night was that little Muttley snicker.

I never took Kevin down, but I guess he had the last laugh; we sold the house and moved.

"He will win who knows when to fight and when not to fight."
[Sun Tzu ~ 544–496 BC ~ Chinese Philosopher]

—Chapter Twenty-Three—

The Golden Shower—2015

Sarah, Carter, Austin & Matt ~ circa 2015

I t's not what you think. Well, it probably is—but in an innocent, yet still repugnant sort of way. Is there simultaneously an innocent and repugnant way? This account is not for the prim and proper, so if you are easily offended, best move on to the next chapter.

This tale takes place on a family trip out west. A fantastic family with a Super-Dad, my Cousin Matt, and his vivacious and often impish wife, Sarah. I say "impish" with impunity, because she is about five-foot-two and a hundred pounds wet. Dressed as an elf this past Christmas, she literally sat on top of the bookcase in their family room — on a shelf. A perfectly staged and classically created hilarious life-sized meme of the "Elf on the Shelf".

These two have whacky stories and have allowed me to borrow this one; it makes me laugh every time I think of it. Strangers in crowds look at me quizzically when I just start laughing out of the blue. I tell them in my best drunken, Dudley Moore Arthur impersonation, "Sometimes I just think funny thoughts... and they make me laugh."

Matt is a teacher with summers off, so he would take his two boys on camping trips across the fruited plain. And just as most brothers do, they had their share of arguments, wrestling, jockeying for the prime seat in the car, not sharing stuff, and one-upmanship. But by and large they were and are, unassailably tight brothers. On this trip however, that bond would be tested.

It was 2015, the boys were tweeners. Austin was twelve-not-quite-thirteen, and Carter had just turned ten. It was a family trip — envision the Griswold's in the movie, Vacation. They weren't in the Family Truckster, but close: the family minivan. This trip was from their home in Chicago, down to the soft white beaches of the Pan Handle in Florida, for a little surf and sun.

The boys had been well behaved the entire ride down, and, after multiple stops, it was getting dark as the family was in the home stretch. Carter had been playing on his Gameboy and Austin was writing in his journal — one that he had been studiously keeping of their myriad travels and exploits over the summer. Sarah and Matt were both tired and ready to be there, get checked in, and kick back with cocktail in hand after the long drive.

Carter was in the seat behind Matt and Austin behind Sarah, who was riding shotgun. The family had stopped for a couple of sodas along the way, but it had been a while since the last rest stop. Carter had to go. Numero uno. A 10-100 on the side. You get the gist. But they were only a half-hour away. "Just hold it —we're almost there," came the edict from the front seat.

Another ten minutes went by and Carter was getting antsy. "Mom, I have to go-ooooo." Austin rolled his eyes, he'd heard this before. But Sarah looked back over her shoulder and could see Carter starting to squirm. Matt jumped in; how hard could this be? "Take the empty cup, and pee in that." Perfect solution, no time lost pulling over and nature's call handled. Pee in the cup, snap the lid back on and throw it away in the first trashcan they came to at the condo.

"Dad! Nooooo." After convincing Carter he could do it and Mom agreeing not to look, he grabbed the cup and setup to take relief. Austin was having no part of any of this and continued focused on his journal. With Mom not looking and Dad cruising down the highway, Carter held his running shorts and underwear down with the thumb of one hand and the cup with the other.

When you're ten years old, and holding it for hours, there's some pressure built up. In normal conditions a kid can arc a stream about twice his height. Fact of anatomical physics. When you're my age, the arc is about half your height. Also, sadly, a fact of anatomical physics. The other unfortunate fact about being young and taking a 10-100, is when you start...you can't stop. Well, whether because this was a nerve-wracking situation or an ill-timed bump in the road, mid-way through, Carter's thumb slipped, and his underwear snapped back.

The stream shot away from the cup towards the ceiling of the van. It happened fast. All of a sudden without warning, Sarah had something warm raining down, matting her long brown hair to her neck and spattering her T-shirt—what in the world? Carter!

Carter couldn't stop—no one can stop. That didn't keep Sarah from screaming at Carter to stop. Matt is trying to keep the car on the road and Austin, who has now had the stream hit his journal, is yelling too, "Mom, he's peeing on my journal! Oh man—it's ruined now," dropping the book like it was a hot potato as Carter tried to redirect back to the cup, in the process dousing himself too.

The golden shower: family style. Not in her wildest dreams did Sarah envision this turn of events. The underwear snap had hit young Carter mid-way, perfectly pinning it at just the right angle to rain down on Sarah and, in a desperate effort to redirect, took out Austin and his journal as collateral damage. Matt went ahead and pulled the minivan over.

After a not-so-pleasant change of clothes on the side of the road for Sarah and Carter, and mopping up of the ceiling, floor, and seats, and the forensic bagging of Austin's journal, they piled back in the car. No need to find a restroom now; Carter was good. The rest of the ride was quiet, as the events of the night settled in infamy.

"If you find it hard to laugh at yourself, I would be happy to do it for you."
[Groucho Marx ~ 1895–1977 ~ American Comedian]

—Chapter Twenty-Four—

Karaoke/Biker Bar—2016

Killing (butchering) Daydream Believer ~ circa 2016

It was a sultry night. After a long day on the links in the Sonoran Desert of California, the atmosphere was rife for overindulgence, decadence, and possibly incarceration. And we were on a slippery slope heading straight for it.

Eight of us weekend warriors were engaged in a three-day golf tournament where stress was at a maximum—not because of a huge payout, but because honor and pride were on the line. For fourteen years, the eight of us would take five days off in late January and play in a boys-trip golf tournament; grueling, but tremendous fun. Typically, the outing took place in Arizona and, thus it was subtitled The Tournament of AZ Holes.

It was a guy's trip, no doubt, and when the tournament was young, there were thirty-six holes of golf in a day, bar-hopping, then friendly poker. As we got up in years it turned into twenty-seven holes and pick your best two nines for eighteen. Next, it became just eighteen, but still bar-hopping, melding into poker until the wee hours. Then it turned into just eighteen, a nice dinner and some poker until the weak drifted off after losing a few hands. Now it's eighteen holes, a nap, dinner, and sleep in front of the TV. *Pathetic*.

For a stint, the tournament moved to Desert Springs, California. And that is where this tale is set. It began with a few harmless beers on the course. That led to a few cocktails when the round was finished. We were in the middle of the tourney, wrapping up day two. Day two is always Mexican night. Mexican means margaritas and margaritas mean tequila. And tequila means the slope just got about twenty degrees steeper. We piled into our minivan rental and hit the town! We used to wear the leather dusters, cowboy boots and hats, the whole nine yards. But now we were in a minivan for goodness sake.

After a jovial night at the local Mexican joint, we were feeling pretty well lubricated and so to not regress into a geriatric golf outing of wimps, we decided to find a manly bar to continue the shenanigans. (All persons in this story have had their names changed to protect their identities; though they are not innocent.) The host of the tournament, Rolph, who lived in Indio at the time knew of a local BBQ/karaoke/pool hall/biker bar establishment. No one was given the opportunity to opt-out. Like the old days; we were all in!

To give background for this local bar, they've got great food. BBQ is exceptional—especially so after a few rounds of Jose Cuervo. We'd just eaten a ton of Mexican and swigged over $300 in margaritas, so we weren't gonna run-up a huge dinner tab. They sport a pretty interesting crowd. Lots of bikers, some cowboy types, a few urban professionals, and leather. Sort of a country vibe to the establishment, but certainly a mix of clientele and, while we didn't stick out, we didn't exactly blend.

The first thing, in hindsight, to note, was the bouncer at the door wanded us for knives and other weapons. They told us no wearing caps sideways or showing colors. This was not a problem, since we wore our hats straight forward and didn't have matching colored outfits, but that's not what he meant; absolutely no gang fighting.

We were a bunch of happy, white-collar stiffs from back east— we're not fighters, we're golfers! That earned not even a polite smile from the very serious, very large, and ripped bouncers even though we used our best Irish and Scottish accents. "Well t'en, shiver me timbers mates, tis a tough crowd." Still nothing.

The second thing to note, was that a fairly large percentage of chicks in this bar were not so attracted to us as they once were. Not sure if we lost our swag somewhere along the way, or if we were just aging out. And we may have been a tad obnoxious, so the rest of the patrons were not laughing as loud at our commentary as we were. We weren't that bad, but, in hindsight, probably could have been a smidge more subdued.

The third thing to note, was that the karaoke singers were not all that bad. And if the folks listening drank a good bit more, We wouldn't sound all that bad either. It's all about song choice and finding a crowd pleaser if you're going to pull the crowd in.

We each went our own direction and began the process of making our mark. A couple of the boys went back to hustle a game of pool. A couple went to throw darts and buy beer to keep the night flowing. A couple just pulled up chairs and soaked it in.

Back in the pool hall, in an effort to impress some of the local ladies, while setting up his cue for a shot, Dan proceeded to come up with a story about being a hand model. These girls were suspicious of this storyline since it sounded as though it could be being made up, out of whole cloth, but went along with it and after a while, bought in completely.

They were cute, young, and gullible. When they learned Dan was also a former nipple model (ret), they were downright intrigued. There were no close inspections in the bar, that we can confirm, but with their curiosity piqued, they indulged the story just to see where it would go.

As Dan expounded on the storied history of his mammilla, Garo started to run the adjacent pool table. He took a couple of the local boys down and was on a pretty good winning streak, when the apparent owner decided it was time for him to give up the table. Garo wasn't going down without a fight though, and so the owner proposed they raise the dollar stakes and play for a T-shirt from the bar.

If the owner won, Garo gave up the table and if Garo won, then he got a fifteen percent discount on the T-shirt—but still had to buy it. Garo is scrappy for sure, but all of 135 lbs. wet and wasn't really spoiling for a knockdown drag-out in a biker bar that checked him for weapons and gang colors anyway—so they played for the T-shirt... discount.

While all this was going on in the back, after blowing the crowd away with my rendition of the Blues Brothers "Hey Bartender," at the karaoke mic, I was coaxing Rolph to get up there and do a duet with me. Rolph had never sung karaoke in public before, but after six rounds of Jose Cuervo, he found his foot tapping along with the beat. I told him to pick any song he would be willing to sing, and he settled on Daydream Believer. I had thrown a few back for sure, but "Daydream Believer?" Did he mean, I'm a Believer by Smashmouth? We could rock that! No, Daydream Believer by the Monkees. Davy Jones, really? Curious, but if it got Rolph up there, I was in!

It was a great setup for karaoke. For duets, they had monitors at either side of the stage, so each performer could see the lyrics without looking down or backwards. As we broke into "Daydream Believer," I looked across Rolph's shoulder to my monitor and he looked across mine to his. To the crowd, it looked as though we were gazing into each other's eyes; "...Cheer up sleepy Jean, oh what can it mean, to a...Daydream believer and a homecoming Quee–ee–ee–een!"

During the course of our tune, a couple of questionable comments had the remainder of our forces marshaling together, so as to not encourage a brawl. There were some modest head nods by a few locals. The bulk of the catcalls came from our own bench. Probably the wittiest throw-off line, eight rounds into Jose Cuervo, was when a rather large woman, who had squeezed into a rather tight pair of leather pants, walked by and Jorge leaning over to Jib and Pate quipped, "The cow looked better in that."

We wrapped up the duet to sustained applause. But it was mostly guys that were clapping—and not so much our own guys. The ladies didn't seem to be fawning much at all. It was actually quite tender singing in the spotlight with Rolph, and with the local boys appreciating the earnestness with which we sang.

It was then we realized we were in a gay bar (this was not only somewhat surprising, but a relief!). All the puzzle pieces fell into place. The leather-clad girls mostly talking to other girls. The stares that we thought we were garnering were not because we were not locals. The overly friendly barkeep that complimented Huck's jeans. After ten rounds of Jose Cuervo, we lost count and started counting again!

It was getting late, and time to think about calling it a night. During the course of events, Huck had taken the minivan back to the Mexican joint to retrieve a pair of forgotten sunglasses, and upon returning had parked in a different spot. Rolph and I were last to leave the bar, stoked from our debut of *Daydream Believer* and, even though we had some difficulty walking a straight line, were certainly capable of driving.

We teetered to the minivan. We weren't sure where the rest of the crew was, but we decided to get in, so Rolph hit the remote a couple times to unlock the doors, and we climbed aboard. I knew we'd been in the bar awhile, but someone had left their stuff in the front seat of our van? It was baby diapers and clothes. Who in the hell changed their baby in the front seat of our van? I started tossing the diapers, wipes and clothes into the back of the van as Rolph tried to get the key in the ignition. Suddenly, we looked at each other and realized simultaneously, we're in the wrong van!

When Rolph had pressed the remote to unlock the doors, apparently a few spaces away our minivan lights blinked on and off as it chirped, unbeknownst to us. The other boys looked on like they were watching a comedy sketch, just laughing at the two idiots who were actually climbing into another van after the lights had just blinked and the horn sounded in the one they were in a few spots away. They didn't shout out to let us know we were climbing in someone else's unlocked van either; they just sat back, laughing, to see how this would play out.

Rolph and I were laughing so hard we couldn't stand up and stumbled away from the wrong van we had climbed into after tossing whoever's stuff in the back, not sure where to go. So Rolph hit the remote again and the van a few spaces away lit up like a Christmas tree—which got us belly laughing all over again! Rolph climbed into the driver's side and I climbed into the passenger side, tears streaming down our faces. After we caught our breath and resumed some semblance of control, I asked Rolph what happened to the other guys?

"We're back here, dumbasses." We didn't even see them when we got in. They had witnessed the whole debacle and were just shaking their heads. And they were still laughing, but clearly not with us. I can neither confirm nor deny, but pretty sure one of them took the keys and drove us back to the hotel.

"There comes a time in the affairs of man when he must take the bull by the tail and face the situation."
[W.C. Fields ~ 1880–1946 ~ Comedian]

—Chapter Twenty-Five—

Something's Fishy—2016

Jack and thousands of eyeless fish near John's Pass,
St. Petersburg Beach ~ 2016

Vacations for my family have often been adventurous. We have
had fantastic vacations, some of them coming unexpectedly,

and some of them planned and played out just the way they were envisioned. Most of them have a hitch or two, but once you're looking back on them you can find the humor and they become the most memorable. Unfortunately, for my family, I may be the curse for doomed vacations and usually the harbinger involves rodents.

Over the years, we became fans of the Pan Handle in Florida, and vacationed there many a time. Our kids now grown, we decided to venture a little farther south for a change. We found a condo on Treasure Island in St. Petersburg and decided to give that a whirl. We had no dramatic condo issues, although, now four adults, we were a bit cramped. But no worries, we'd be on the beach and at the local establishments anyway.

The first night, we found a local eatery called The Hut Bar and Grill, just over the bridge in John's Pass Village and Boardwalk. It was an open restaurant overlooking Boca Ciega Bay with a cover band playing. We ordered a round of Margaritas; it was Jimmy Buffet songs after all. We were relaxed with our guard down and unsus-pecting—that's when the omen came. Something small, furry, and quick scampered across Maureen's flip-flop clad foot.

Now, Maureen likes all animals large and small, but not out of the shadows in a restaurant, while listening to a Jimmy Buffet cover band. After some discussion about what to do, the waitress wide-eyed with a little shock, offered a round on the house, so we had double shots of tequila, strictly for psychological/medicinal purposes. By the time the food came, our appetites had waned, although it didn't really stop me from eating heartily. That was night one.

The next day we hung out at the beach and were chilling in our beach chairs, cocktails in hand, having a great family vacation. We played bocce ball as a family many times over the years and had brought a set to the beach. As we played up and down the sand, we began have to dodge around a few dead fish. Kind of gross, but, it's a beach, fish die. Right?

Then as we strolled down the beach to find a local joint for lunch we could walk up to, we noticed more dead fish. Strangely, lots of them. By the second day, there were thousands of them. By the third day, hundreds of thousands of fish rotting and smelling like we were in the bowels of a giant garbage disposal. Every single fish, and I mean every single one of them, had their eyes pecked out by colonies of seagulls. It was like we were in an insane Hitchcock movie! What in the world was going on? Apparently, most of the nutrients in fish are in the eyes. Who knew?

By day four, we didn't have to be hit over the head with a dead fish to learn we were at the epicenter of a Florida red-tide, as literally millions of fish washed ashore. Red-tide is a concentration of a naturally occurring algae bloom that produces powerful breve-toxins, which kills marine life and can cause respiratory irritation among beachgoers.

I'm not sure what brevetoxins are, but the root word toxin was really all we needed to know. Great timing on switching to St. Petersburg. I should have known it when that rodent scurried across Maureen's foot. Decision time; do we stay and tough it out or pay to stay in two places at the same time? We had all taken off work, so postponing wasn't really an option. Risk respiratory illness, stay inside a small condo with the sun shining bright outside or get out of Dodge? We packed up and moved the vacation to San Destin, where we savored burgers, pasta, and chicken.

Our vacations don't usually devolve into horror stories, but they often come close. Is it just me? Now that a year-and-a-half has gone by, we can look back and laugh. You have to or else you'd never take another one.

"A vacation is what you take when you can no longer take what you've been taking."
[Earl Wilson ~ 1907–1987 ~ American Journalist]

—Chapter Twenty-Six—

Just Another Day on the Links—2017

Chestatee Golf Course No 17 Par 3 ~ Sept 1, 2017

I t was a perfect fall day: September 1, 2017. There was a steady breeze under sunny skies, almost no humidity, and it was about eighty degrees. Perfect for a round of golf with my weekend warrior comrades. Or at least, acquaintances — some of them don't like to be lumped in with my ilk, so for the purposes of this anecdote I'll call them: Ralph, Gary, Pat, and George.

Gary had setup for a little two-day tournament, to enjoy a couple of rounds of golf and get our respective spouses and what we could of our families together, over Labor Day weekend. The round started as our rounds usually do: like the Pro's. We each hit *two* balls off the first tee—and a "choosigan" (not to be confused with a mulligan in which you must take your second ball even if it results in a lie worse than the first ball). A choosigan, you get to choose which shot to hit—just like the Pro's.

Of the eight balls hit by the first four guys, only one came to rest in the fairway with four lost, the balance in the rough or woods. (See excerpt at end of this anecdote from my forthcoming book, this is covered in: Chapter 2—How to Hit a Nike from the Rough, When You Hit a Titleist from the Tee.) The most unlikely to par this first hole was George, who had a handicap of 28.5, but who was off to a good start and sank the putt to jump out to an early lead. After one hole.

The day progressed well with all of us in the hunt, shooting better than we usually do, with no real blowups until the ninth hole. While Ralph and I would go on to par the hole, Pat would hole out with a quadruple bogey nine and Gary, with a snowman (the golf nomenclature for an eight). (From my forthcoming book this is covered in: Chapter 1—How to Properly Line Up Your Fourth Putt.)

Even with thirty-four strokes hit on the hole collectively, we moved along quickly, we had to since we had grouped together about the third hole and were playing as a fivesome. (This is covered in: Chapter 5—When to Give the Marshal the Finger). Keeping it light, I quipped, "Who hits first; the eight or the nine?" Ralph, Gary and I all had a chuckle.

On the tenth hole things went a little awry. Actually, it started while driving to the tenth hole. There's a pretty steep hill coming down to that tee box, and Ralph and Gary were the lead golf cart with George in the middle cart and Pat and I bringing up the rear. George was texting, although he would immediately deny this while he quickly put his phone down, and not looking forward as he came down the hill and when he looked up realized the cart in front had stopped.

Ralph had just stepped out of the cart, but Gary was still halfway in it when the carts crashed in spectacular fashion. Golf paraphernalia, drinks, clubs, balls all went flying, including Gary as he was ejected. George claimed the breaks had failed, which was possibly true, so from that point forward we let George take the lead just to be safe. Needless to say, both struggled with their drives on that hole—Gary's balance impeded from the bruise on his hamstring where the seat guard had impacted him, and George's normal game got in his way. (This is covered in: Chapter 15—How to Relax When You Are Hitting Five off the Tee.)

The atmosphere started getting a little more serious as we came into the final six holes, Gary was limping down the homestretch— literally. With handicap, George was well on his way to winning the day, and possibly the tournament. Pat was up and down like a yo-yo, but in the hunt, and Ralph was solid as always. This could not stand; George playing the lowest round of his life after taking out Gary and still beating us. (Covered in: Chapter 6—Using Your Shadow on the Greens to Maximize Earnings.)

I finished the front nine with five out of seven pars, which is really good for me. I had struggled on the back nine as I came to the final three holes. After a string of bogies and double-bogies, that's when the tide turned. The best three consecutive holes in my storied golfing career of thirty-seven years were about to unfold.

Number sixteen is a long par five with a split fairway where you could lay-up past a stand of trees to safely reach the green in three, or you could cut a corner over a series of five bunkers and go for it in two. I had boomed my drive and opted to go for it in two, which would require a solid three-rescue club, with uphill and wind— about a 210-yard shot.

I hit it flush and put it on the right side of the green in two; putting for Eagle (that's two under par if any non-golf readers have made it this far into the story). The problem was the pin was a good fifty feet away on the left side of a back-to-front sloped green. I took my time, lined-up the putt, and gave it a whack. It was uphill/side-hill and broke about seven feet.

As it came off the highpoint of the side-hill line, drifting back down towards the hole, I missed the cup by about ten inches and it trundled on by about eight feet. It looked good for so long and then just missed! Contrary to my usual following putt when I've done this, I made the eight foot come-backer for birdie and left sixteen feeling pretty good.

Number seventeen is a downhill par three. Tough hole, because of the dramatic elevation change, the green some forty feet below the tee and guarded by bunkers left and right. With having just scored a birdie, I was first to hit on the next tee box. Typically, we refer to this condition as ripe for a PBFU. Post Birdie [Foul] Up. The tee box was up, and playing 137 yards, downhill into a freshening breeze.

After debating clubs, I smoothed my forty-six-degree pitching wedge. Hit that baby right on the sweet spot. As it hit the apex of its trajectory, I commented to Ralph that I wasn't sure I had enough club. He said it looked right to him. The ball came down landing twelve inches short of the hole, took one tiny hop and rolled in for a *Hole-in-One!* It was a shot I'll never forget! Since I have a reputation for slight embellishment on occasion in some of my story telling, I did have all present sign the scorecard attesting the round (below).

Number eighteen is a hard finishing hole—a long uphill par four with a narrow, deep and severely undulating green. I wasn't done yet. A slightly wayward drive—let's call it a power fade—left me with an uphill shot that required another fade to reach in two. The wind was in my face, and so going to my caddie and cart-partner, Pat, I asked how many extra clubs I should hit to make sure I reached. We guessed between two and three clubs worth of wind and uphill. I hit four-iron from about 170 and landed on the back tier of the green. The pin was way up front.

Pat is no longer my caddie.

That left me a sixty-five foot putt back down an undulating green with about a three-foot drop two-thirds of the way to the hole for birdie. I knew I'd be posting the scorecard and after hitting the hole-in-one, the last thing I wanted to do was follow it up with a bogey. Great. I took my time reading the put—rephrase: I had plenty of time waiting for the others to get on the green to read my putt. I had recently watched an interview with Jordan Spieth on how he reads his putts and took to heart his methodology. I looked at it from four sides and walked to the crown of the hill to find the fall-line to hole.

From my calculations it had about eleven or twelve inches of break to the top of the hill, then would straighten out as it fell towards the hole. The grass was "striped" from being mowed and if I could hit the ball about halfway through the width of the stripe in the first forty feet of the putt, and just slow it at the top of the hill, it should then gather speed and track down the fall-line right to the hole. No problem here.

Ralph tended the flagstick as I settled over the putt and looked at the putt in thirds, just as Spieth said, and picked a spot to hit to. I struck the putt firm and, as it got to the crown on the green, just started down the hill gathering speed. Ralph said something to the effect of, "Holy [cow]! That's going in..." and pulled the pin as the ball dropped dead-center of the hole for birdie!

That was almost as exciting as the hole-in-one. To hit the first hole-in-one AND finish birdie-eagle-birdie, is the highlight of my golfing career and I am almost one-hundred percent certain I'll never repeat that. But I'll sure as hell try. The best part, honestly though, was having four really good friends there to witness and share in the story. I'd never even seen a live hole-in-one roll into the cup in person. And now I own one. It was a perfect fall day: September 1, 2017.

The boys decided this was not skill and instead blind luck, stopping by a convenience store and forcing me to pick numbers for several lotto tickets for the mega millions. We all put in ten dollars and agreed to split whatever winnings there were to be. Just think what you could do with one-fifth of two-hundred million bucks — before taxes. We watched the numbers be drawn that night and split the winning tickets — eight dollars between us. $1.60 each. Sweet! ... we only lost $8.40 each.

The Attested Scorecard ~ Sept 1, 2017

"It's good sportsmanship to not pick up lost golf balls while they are still rolling."
[Mark Twain ~ 1835–1910 ~ American Author]

A preview of my forthcoming book: We Call it Golf

Chapter 1 - How to Properly Line Up Your Fourth Putt.

Chapter 2 - How to Play a Nike from the Rough, When You Hit a Titleist from the Tee.

Chapter 3 - How to Avoid the Water When You Lie 8 in a Bunker.

Chapter 4 - How to Get More Distance off the Shank.

Chapter 5 - When to Give the Marshal the Finger.

Chapter 6 - Using Your Shadow on the Greens to Maximize Earnings.

Chapter 7 - When to Implement Handicap Management.

Chapter 8 - Proper Excuses for Drinking Cold beer before 9:00 a.m.

Chapter 9 - How to Rationalize a Six-Hour Round.

Chapter 10 - When Does A Divot Become Classified As Sod.

Chapter 11 - How to Find That Ball That Everyone Else Saw Go into the Water.

Chapter 12 - Why Your Spouse Doesn't Care That You Birdied the 5th.

Chapter 13 - Using Curse Words Creatively to Control Ball Flight.

Chapter 14 - When to Let a Foursome Play through Your Twosome.

Chapter 15 - How to Relax When You Are Hitting Five off the Tee.

—Chapter Twenty-Seven—

Pairing-up—2018

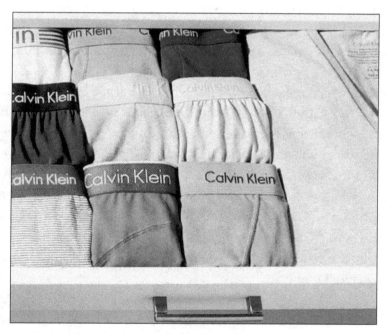

This could easily be my underwear drawer... ~ circa 2018

This is not an earthshattering saga, it will win no poet laureate, nor Nobel prize in literature. But it did crack me up. And so, to virtual pen and paper I imparted:

Over the years, I have struggled with finding the right style and fit for underwear. See, this narrative is not gonna change the world for the better. I have a closet full of misfits, or wedgie-inducing discards, or underwear that was perfect until washed one time and now can only fit a Ken doll. And Ken has *no package* so even that is a point of contention! I bet I've tried twenty different styles: briefs, boxers, boxer-briefs, low-rise, full-rise, sport, cotton, Lycra-polyester blend, microfiber stretch—you get the idea. Obsessed. And never pacified.

My wife, Maureen, has put up with this tomfoolery for over thirty years. Everyone has their thing; this is one of mine. I have other things, possibly more embarrassing but not as intimate. I think.

To interject some backstory: once, about a decade ago, I had taken a new job at Carter's/OshKosh and had a new boss, Robin. She has long since become a great friend, and on this occasion, we were setting a baby shop up in Miami Dadeland. The day before we were to fly out, I had finally found what I thought was the perfect fit of Calvin Klein's and, because I was a frugal purchaser, would only buy on sale with a double discount. This particular style of tighty-whities was flying off the shelves, so I went to a local Macy's to scarf-up the last of what they had. When I got there, they were out of my size. Of course.

So, after haggling and checking other stores, a very helpful associate found eight pairs in the right size, and she could have them shipped to Atlanta. With her trying to locate these all over the country, it had taken way longer than buying a couple pairs of underwear should take, so I was like, "Fine, just have them sent and I'll make another trip back (for underwear!) to the store and pick them up." But as it turns out, she had to go through a distribution center to place the order, blah-blah-blah and another thirty minutes past by. She mentioned in passing they were coming from the Miami Dadeland store in Florida.

Realizing I would be there the next day, I had her put them on hold and I would just grab them when I was down there. Perfect. Except, I didn't think through the fact that I was with my new female boss on our first business trip and I couldn't very well disguise them, since I would have nothing except a see-through plastic Macy's bag to put them in.

So as, we finished, I told Robin I needed to run and purchase something at Macy's. We were leaving, so eventually after a little probing, I came clean why I was buying underwear at this Macy's vs. Atlanta and after all they were at half-off, discounted another forty percent and these were the only ones in my size left. She was laughing and said, "By all means, then — go! Can't pass this up."

When I came back to where she was waiting for me to return from my purchase, she had our whole department on a conference call, and I knew from the tears streaming down her face that it would be a long time before I lived this one down. Let me just say, sometimes it's best to just let the sale go.

Fast forward eleven years to 2018. Now in another line of work and contemplating some options on frame displays I am making for a client, I was thinking out loud while absent-mindedly folding some underwear. Maureen was getting dressed for the day, overhearing me mumble to myself. I was contemplating how to take two versions of the same thing for this client and combine them into one display. "If these two guys go together," I was muttering, "how would that work? I could put them side by side or do I stack them?"

161

Maureen seeing me folding underwear while saying this, started laughing, "So your underwear are friends now? Which guys should pair together? Now they're 'guys?'" She was like, "You have some serious issues."

Hey, there's a lot going on in our lives and if she has to deal with one more 'whacko,' it wouldn't surprise her. No one really prepares for their spouse to start talking to their underwear like they were giving advice to a dear friend. And knowing my history, it wasn't that much of a stretch to assume I was pairing up my underwear based on style, fabric, whatever; especially since it was a seemingly soft-spoken and intimate conversation.

There is nothing better than a hysterical misinterpretation of two innocent and unrelated events to engender a huge and seemly unstoppable belly laugh. If I could have one good laugh like that a day, I'd live to be a hundred!

"A day without laughter is a day wasted."
[Charlie Chaplin ~ 1888–1977 ~ English Actor]

—Chapter Twenty-Eight—

Man's Best Friend?—2018

Annie at her post ~ December, 2018

I have been married thirty years now. My wife, Maureen, has owned a dog or two—or three—at a time, since she rescued her first one thirty-four years ago in the summer of 1984. This should give you a good idea of the pecking order in our household. She

163

has owned dogs longer than she has owned me. If there is reincarnation, you want to come back as one of Maureen's dogs.

I am a dog lover as well—we always had them as I grew up. My father was a great trainer of dogs. Hunting, yes, but we always had a pet dog too, usually a Golden Retriever or some kind of Labrador. But, I am not the kind of dog lover Maureen is. I love them when they're well trained and stay outside without begging or whining, and when they're not barking at squirrels. I love them when they sit or heel when you tell them to. I love them when they're older and a little calmer and not jumping on you with muddy paws or using the family-room carpet as their toilet. Maureen loves them *unconditionally*.

There are some decisions you look back on in life, which set the course inalterably, for better or for worse. Maureen and I had been dating about ten months in the summer of '84. Her childhood dog had died that Spring and she was dropping hints about getting a dog. We were still testing each other's boundaries at that point, since she had considerably more experience in dating—seeing as she was my first real girlfriend, I wasn't about to rock the boat.

My family was a big sailing family back in the day, one of my Dad's boats was an eighteen-foot catamaran that we usually hauled down to Panama City Beach a couple times a year. It was a beautiful summer day. The boat was at my folk's house that summer and they decided to take it up the Lake Sidney Lanier (one of the largest man-made lakes in the Southeast, named after the Civil War veteran and Georgia-born poet) just north of Atlanta.

I let Maureen know we were going sailing for the day with my folks up at the lake. Maureen let me know that we were going to get her a dog down at the Humane Society. It wasn't really our first fight, as much as an arguable difference of plans and priorities. I was completely reasonable, explaining that it was a perfect day for a sail with the wind at a good fifteen to twenty knots out of the south-west and getting the boat up to the lake took a bit of scheduling and we could get a dog any day. She explained that I could go sail with my parents and her Dad would take her to get her dog.

As we drove to the Humane Society, I reflected on the fact that even though she pulled the "if you won't my dad will" card, we could really go for a sail any ol' time. Maureen didn't pull that trump card often, but that first time I knew it wasn't a bluff either. Being the youngest of five children and the only daughter, her dad would do just about anything for her. I was fast learning to pick my battles carefully.

We arrived at the Humane Society and looked over the pups they had. Maureen loves all puppies and most dogs, but one tiny, quiet, black Lab caught her eye. All the other puppies were bouncing and yipping, but this one was remarkably calm and when she picked him up, he just quietly laid his head on her shoulder. Uh oh.

I told Maureen, he was sure sweet, but he was melancholy, because he had to be sick. She needed to find another puppy that had more pep; puppies were not supposed to be so quiet. I picked up lots of cute little puppies and held them, at arm's length, in front of her to choose from. This one could end up costing her a fortune, or she might have to go through the heartbreak of having it put it down.

As we drove home from the Humane Society with that little black Lab on her lap, she decided to name it Jake. Jake was a really good puppy, and Jake was, in fact, sick. He had Kennel cough and mild mange and I'm sure some other parasite or another. He cost a good penny more than anticipated with all the shots and vet bills, but we had him for a good sixteen years and he did prove to be a really good dog. Hardest thing I've ever done was take him to the vet that final time.

Maureen and Jake ~ circa, Summer of 1984

Since then, we've had some seven dogs, sometimes as many as three at a time. On September 15 of 2018 our fifteen-year-old dog, Riley, moved on to greener pastures, running unencumbered in her celestial habitation. Maureen and I had been discussing eventually getting a one- or two-year old dog, already house trained but not too old for new tricks, preferably male. We were both in agreement on this. Puppies are a lot of work, and we're beyond that level of commitment.

I advocated for a medium-sized dog, golden or yellow so dark fur wouldn't litter the house. I could live with that. Maybe after the first of the year, once we'd had a few months respite without a dog, for the first time in our married lives, we'd go look for a new member of the family. Good plan.

Not ten days later on Maureen's birthday, she stated she was on her way to look at dogs. Too soon! It's too soon, I implored, but even I could see how this was going end. Thirty-four years ago, I learned to pick my battles. The Hobie Cat is long gone and I have no access to a sailboat of any kind. We (meaning me) once again went over the kind of dog we discussed as she nodded and smiled knowing-ly—a twinkle in her eye. I have learned to dread that twinkle.

A few hours later, "This is Annie." A six-month-old, untrained, dark haired, female puppy. Maureen set her down so I could meet her. One loving glance, okay, and slight groan, from me and she immediately peed on the floor. Deep breaths. They say a dog is man's best friend. This little dog is not man's best friend. She is Maureen's best friend.

Change of subject; why name her Annie? Sweet Annie from the Zac Brown song? Or little orphan Annie? Both good guesses, but Annie gets her name from Maureen's Mom who was one-hundred percent Irish, and as it turns out, the dog was born on St Patrick's Day. Fate. I reluctantly, under great duress and formal objection, agreed to "*try*" her for two weeks... three months ago (as of this writing).

Now she sleeps in our bed. In the middle. She snores. She zooms around in circles. Up the stairs—down the stairs. Over the furni-ture. On the furniture. All at 100 mph. She thinks she's cute. She is pushing one of her stupid paws at me right now wanting to play. We think she is a Belgian Malinois, of the Belgian Shepherd breed—the same dog the U.S. Secret Service uses to guard the grounds of the White House. So we've got that going for us.

In spite of my inclinations, she has started to win me over, just a smidge! She has settled into her role and place in the family as she explores how to manipulate us, testing her boundaries at every opportunity. She sits vigilantly atop the stairs of our back deck, keeping watch over the yard for squirrels to chase, who dare to enter her domain, or for deer to charge, then just as quickly retreat from, who eye her indifferently, while munching on leaves from the other side of our fence.

She has become an expert hunter, tracker, and killer of cockroaches who seek refuge from the cold or rain. None of us want the task of taking out cockroaches, least of all my daughter, who cannot abide spiders, cockroaches, or any small insects—for this Annie has earned our respect. Their carcasses turn up intermittently, usually on their backs, incriminating claw marks in the carpet where she had tormented them thinking them playthings.

She has brought the obligatory dead bird and laid it at the back door. We relish the day she gets her first chipmunk or mole—those are always really pleasant to receive. I am certain there will be other tales of Annie's antics. Until then, we know she'll be doggedly on guard, unless we throw a ball.

"No one appreciates the very special genius of your conversation as the dog does."
[Christopher Morley ~ 1890–1957 ~ American Author]

Acknowledgements

I t is here I must again thank Maureen, my wife, who has laughed along side of me as our life has played itself out. Through good times and hard times, retaining the ability to laugh has made the hard times less hard and kept our perspective on what really matters.

Also, again to my children Jack and Maddie, who are the subjects of many of these anecdotes and who have themselves developed fantastic senses of humor. Walt Disney's quote is a perfect reflection for both kids: *"Laughter is timeless. Imagination has no age. And dreams are forever."*

And to my father, who lived and heard many of these tales but, never got to read them as Parkinson's slowly robbed him of body and mind until he won the long-fought battle, in October of 2018 — the year this book was compiled.

To all my family and many friends who have cajoled, pushed, persuaded, and berated me into putting all these stories first in writing and then into this collection of Toileture™ — specifically and dogmatically, my Aunt Bonnie. Without all of their constant encouragement, I doubt any of this would have ever seen the light. I have many more stories in the cue if you enjoyed these, and will hopefully be releasing the next volume in late 2019, as well as *The Eigel Christmas Epistles—the rest of the story.*

And to Liberty Hill Publishing and Salem Author Services, without whom this book would not have been published, but remaining an obscure blog and snippets in a series of unknown Christmas letters.

Finally, and most importantly, I would like to thank Almighty God for giving me this small degree of "talent" and surrounding me with folks who both encouraged and supported this endeavor—both inspirationally and financially.

"Drag your thoughts away from your troubles...
by the ears, by the heels, or any other way you can manage it."
[Mark Twain ~ 1835–1910 ~ American Author]

About the Author

J. Christopher Eigel

C hristopher grew up loving the likes of Lewis Grizzard and Paul Harvey and has a passion for the written word. Starting in 1996, he began writing an annual letter at Christmas to be the antithesis of the typical letters that arrive at that time of year, full of boring stories bragging on their families and their litany of vacations taken that year. Self-deprecating humor and sarcasm would be the impetus of his Christmas letter stories: real, embellished, or made-up out of whole cloth..

Eventually, the anecdotes in the Eigel Christmas Epistles became something family and friends eagerly awaited, wanting to see what stories unraveled and what shame or insight was brought to his family. After much prodding and pushing, the author took it to the next level and expounded on those anecdotes with backstory and better context in the form of a series of blog stories. Some of those are collected in this book, many are still to come.

In addition to what Christopher has called this first book in a series: *Toileture*^{TM}, he has written a biographical novella about his Father-in-law's experiences up to and through WWII, including the remarkable reuniting of four separated brothers following the Battle of the Bulge titled: *18 Hours in Liège—A Soldier's Story*. It will be released in late-2019.

Christopher and his wife, Maureen, reside in Roswell, GA with their dog, Annie. Their two children are grown and embarking on their own careers—making their own stories.

[faint] Praise for The Lighter Side of Life

"Baby boomers to millennials who appreciate sarcasm will laugh out loud at the stories and often relatable life experiences of Eigel, as they are representative of American life."

—SALEM AUTHOR SERVICES Editorial Review

"This book was not reviewed nor read by JEFF FOXWORTHY. He probably would not have liked it."

—Anonymous

"Eigel dishonors the legacy of Star Trek and tarnishes the iconic uniform of a Starship Captain."

—What WILLIAM SHATNER likely would have said
had he seen the Author photo

"I love these stories, they are so well crafted. I don't like the drinking parts though; why do you have to tell those parts?"

—SUZANNE, Eigel's Mom

"I haven't read these yet… I lived them, why do I have to read them?"

—MAUREEN, Eigel's Wife